Sometimes inefficiency in a part of a system makes the whole system more effective.

三角折り紙の本

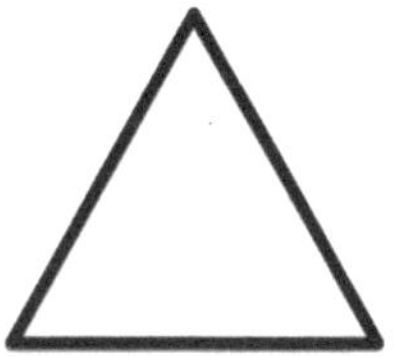
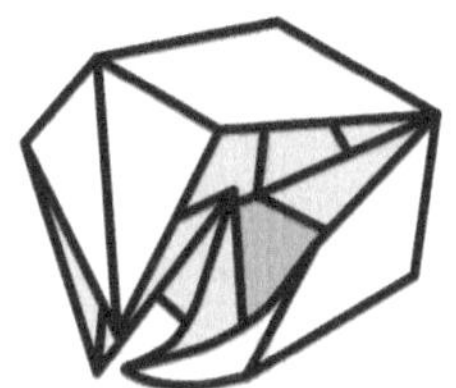

Triangle Origami Book

folding paper in creative and useful ways
inspired by triangles

second edition

with Diagrams and Commentary including
divers decorative and functional
Original Designs
by William Zicker

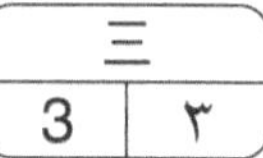

Table of Contents

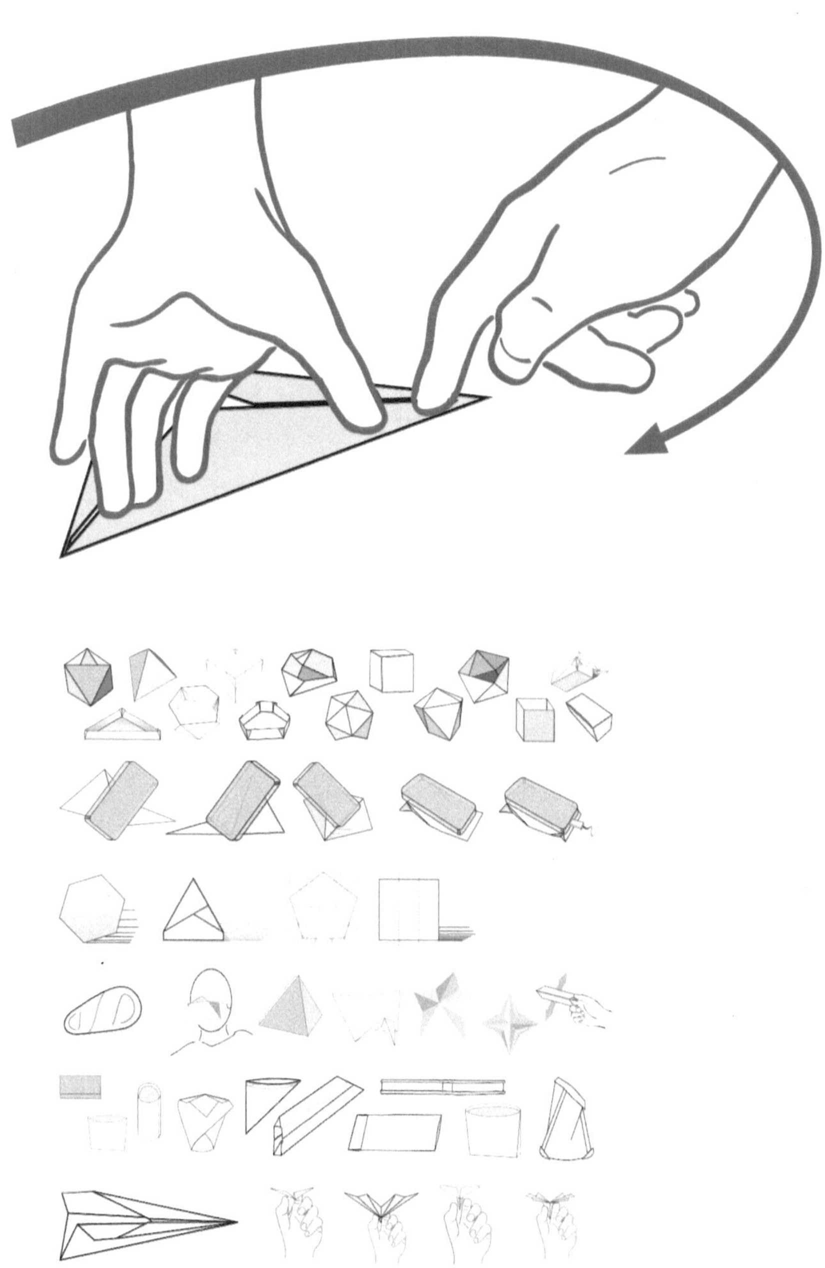

Exodus
"he that gathered much had nothing over, and he that gathered little had no lack"

Proverbs
"Labour not to be rich:
cease from thine own wisdom"

Luke
"But rather seek ye the kingdom of God; and all these things shall be added unto you."

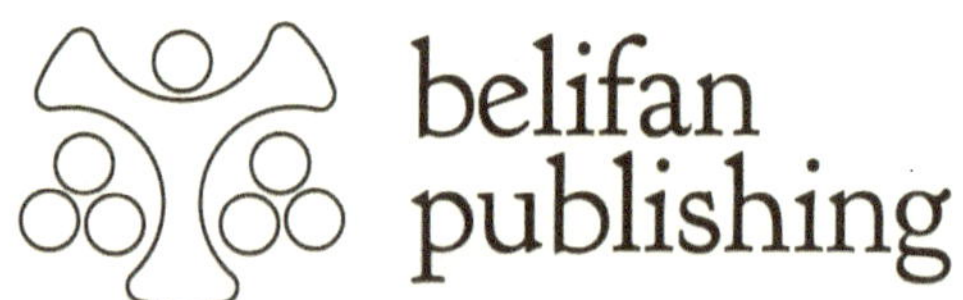

ISBN 978 0 9842655 3 4

First Edition published 2025
Second Edition published 2026

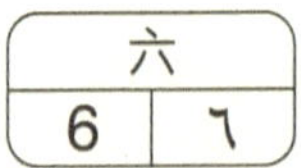

R

Introduction

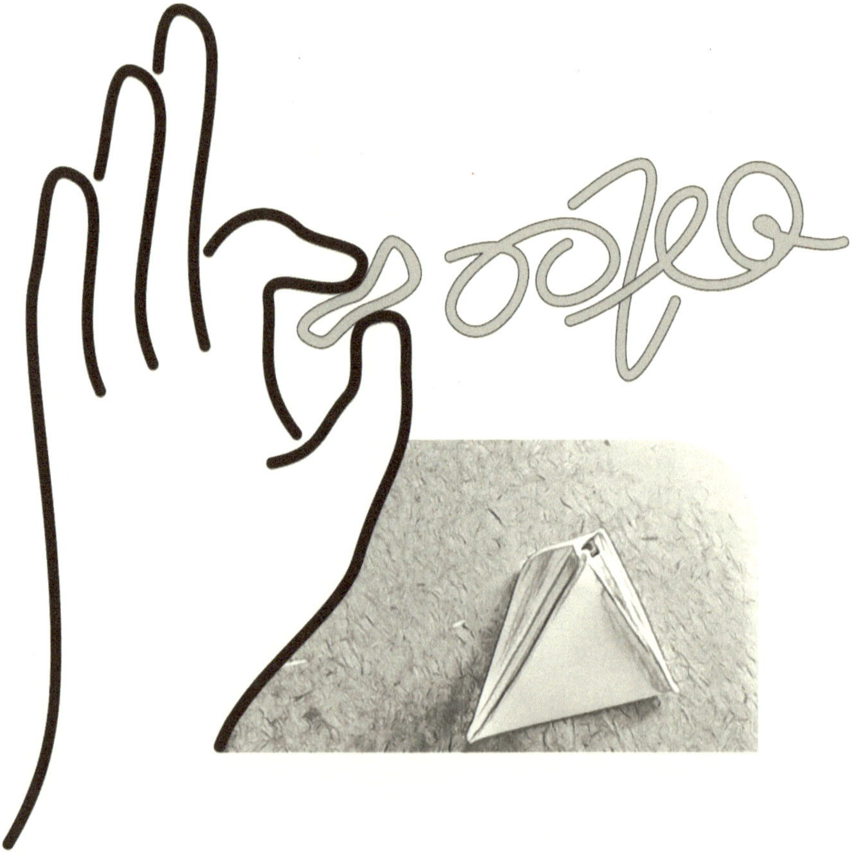

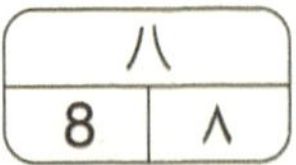

Inventions played an important part in the creation of this book. My first invention was an original origami paper airplane I folded around age ten. At the time origami diagrams made no sense to me.

Many inventions and two patents later, my starch based dilatant composition, Oozeq, needed a biodegradeable paper package. An hour of twisting and squishing paper turned into an interesting little pyramid. It seemed like there was some pattern in the way the paper wrapped around on itself. Multiple hours of reverse engineering and refinement resulted in my second original origami design.

Sharing this pyramid with experienced origami designers, it became evident that I had designed something new. Encouraged to submit this for publication, I found it necessary to diagram the design using a shared standard set of symbols in a generally recognizable format. My efforts are documented in my diagram number 00, Open

Triangular Antiprism from Equilateral Triangle, and number 01, Tetrahedron from Triangular Open Antiprism.

Designing an origami diagram first hand proved useful, as there is so much being communicated. Learning about the Yoshizawa–Randlett system of diagramming allowed me to craft the visual presentation directly, making nuanced and subjective design decisions. This also developed my understanding of the mechanics of origami, leading to further original designs.

The diagram for my first design—number 13, Paper Airplane from Rectangle—finally arrived some 40 years late and was published in the Pacific Coast OrigamiUSA Conference 2023 collection, page 11.

Triangles bind the designs presented here with a common thread. Some are obviously based on a single equilateral triangle, while others are inspired by or incorporate some aspect of a triangular form.

While we're on the topic of two dimensional geometric shapes, hexagons are going to be the next big thing—they're going to be everywhere. That's what I was saying years ago, and now the trend has arrived. Hexagons were not easy to find in arts and crafts stores in 2017. This then uncommon shape, built of triangles, presented a fun opportunity for original origami designs.

Mathematics is the ideal path to determine the largest regular hexagon that can be drawn inside a square. Avoiding math, I worked through a process of guessing and folding, unfolding and tweaking, and a pattern gradually emerged. My trial and error folding eventually arrived at the same conclusion as basic geometry. In the process I documented a series of folds, in half and half again, and the hidden symmetry of my hexagon design emerged.
Shuzo Fujimoto of Japan, 1922-2015,

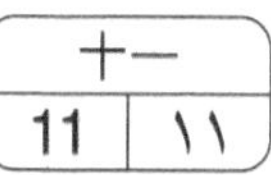

engineered many original designs including a direct alternative to my hexagon design. Where his design calculated an angled fold to define the edges of the hexagon, I stumbled upon a combination of perpendicular and parallel folds halfway between previously defined points. Folding things in half and in half again seems an elegant and accurate method for defining where folds should be made. Perhaps others will be interested in this approach, documented in my diagram number 38, Maximal Hexagon from Square.

Even pentagons can be defined as intersections of X and Y at intervals of halves. Talk about not obvious, this one barely made any sense at all.

Sometimes it's easier to create new things without the tools and methods that arrived at old things. Geometry arrived at old ways of folding a regular pentagon from a square. Building on my strengths, I once again took the path that avoided math and searched for some pattern in half and half again grid lines. Took some time and required some concentration to remember why seemingly arbitrary intersections in the grid were circled. Running through the sketches a few times eventually saw the diagram begin to make sense. While other ways may get similar results, Pentagon Halves and Intersections documented in my diagram number 20 presents an accurate regular pentagon that starts with folding a square of paper in half followed by equally straightforward subsequent steps. I'm starting to see patterns in all this geometry.

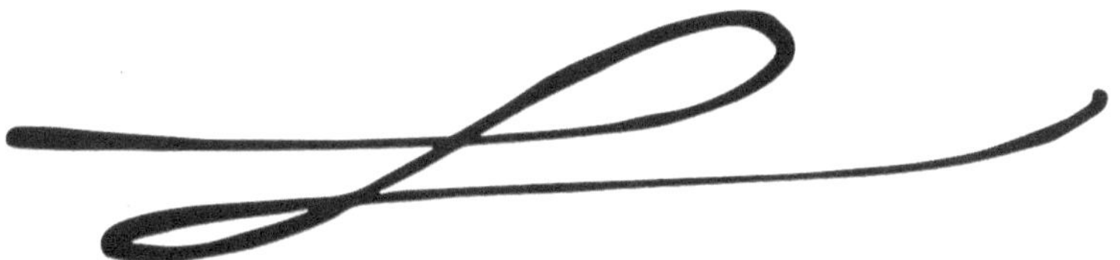

Je n'ai fait celle-ci plus longue que parce que je n'ai pas eu le loisir de la faire plus courte.
Blaise Pascal
Provincial Letters: Letter XVI, 4 December, 1656.
I only made this one longer because I didn't have the time to make it shorter.

Diagrams

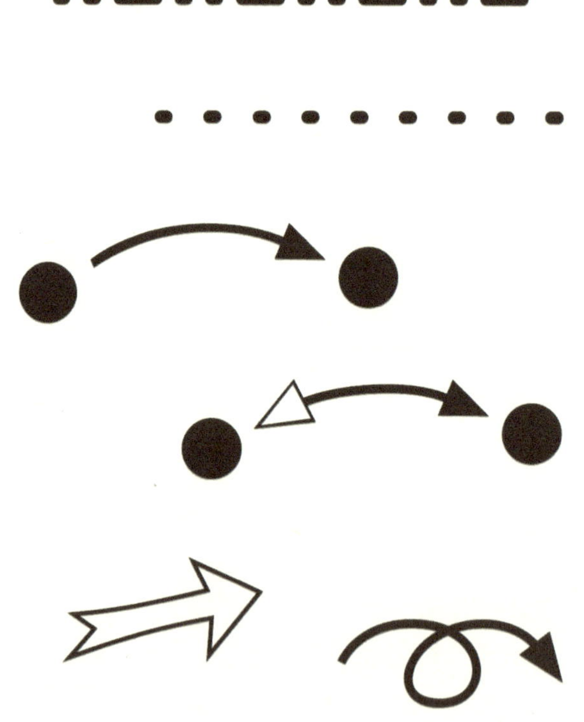

Folds are the basic units of origami. Arrows instruct the movement of paper into folds.
Dashes are longer than dots.
The first line shown opposite is a dashed line. This indicates a valley fold that falls down into the paper.
A mountain fold is shown next, rising up from the paper, comprising two dots and one dash in a repeating pattern.
Solid arrowheads indicate to where paper should move. Adding an outlined arrowhead on the other end shows that the paper is to be unfolded after folding, leaving a crease as a reference point for subsequent folds.
Unfolded creases are denoted in subsequent frames of the diagram as an evenly dotted line with no dashes.
Round dots or similar marks may specify exactly the two points being brought together by the present fold.
Fully outlined wide arrows are used to show a pushing or tucking movement.
As a form takes shape, it may need to be reoriented, flipped over or spun around.
A loop arrow directs the paper be lifted and flipped, so the underside becomes the top side.

The three axis lines show arc arrows, illustrating rotation on either the X/Y, X/Z or Y/Z plane. The next 3/4 circle arrow presents a number of degrees of rotation on the X/Y plane, the surface of the paper.

The last item illustrated is a set of brackets, an attempt on my part to illustrate zooming in, enlarging the drawing from one side of the brackets to the other.

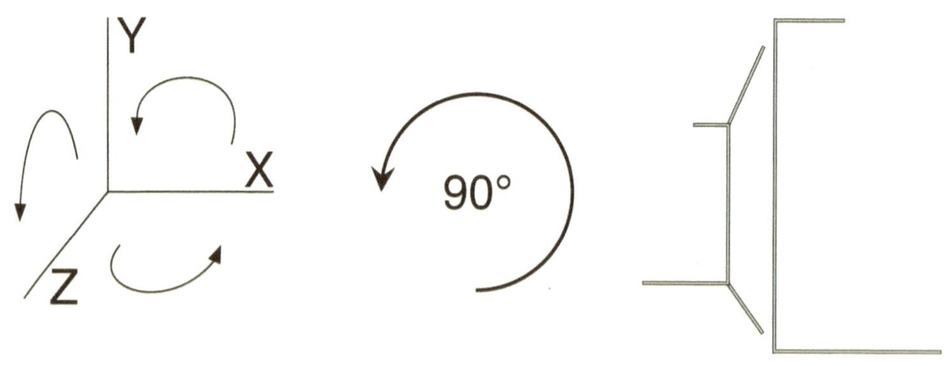

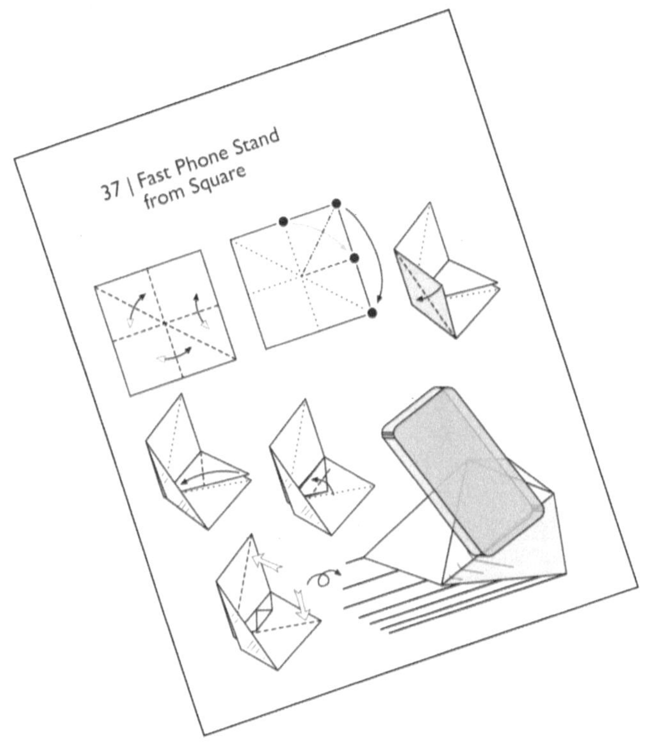

Here is an example of one of the diagrams from this collection.
Title information appears on the top of the page, next to the design number.
A sequence of images are organized loosely in rows from top to bottom, with each step in the process illustrated in each image from left to right.
An illustration of the finished piece is shown at the bottom of the page.

Prisms, Antiprisms and Boxes

Prism is from the Greek word πρίσμα prisma, which originally referred to a piece cut off with a saw. Imagine a tree branch, or a brick. If you were to saw off one end, you would have a cross section. The tree branch might be mostly round like a cylinder, and the piece cut off with a saw would have that same round profile, with a circle shaped surface on each end. Similarly, if the end of a brick was cut off by a saw, the piece would share the brick's squared profile, and each end would have the same square shape of the cross section.

Geometry has adopted this word, which now commonly refers to a three dimensional form with that kind of shape. The profile or cross section of a prism in geometry is a polygon, with the three dimensional form extruded straight out from that two dimensional surface.

An antiprism is like a prism with a twist, where one end cross section is rotated relative to the other. An open prism or open antiprism is a hollow form, with one end open like a tray or box.

00 | Open Triangular Antiprism from Equilateral Triangle

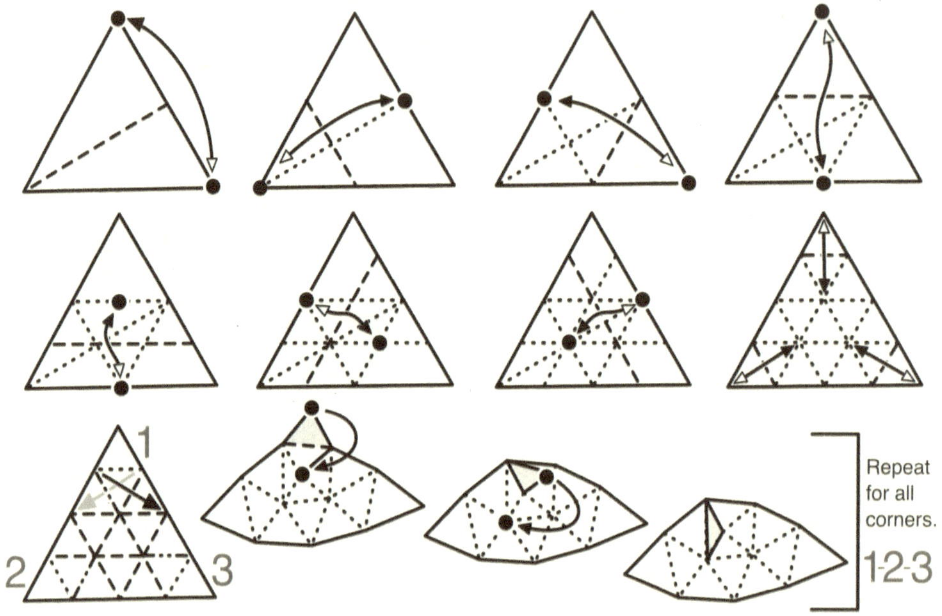

1

2

3

Repeat for all corners.

1-2-3

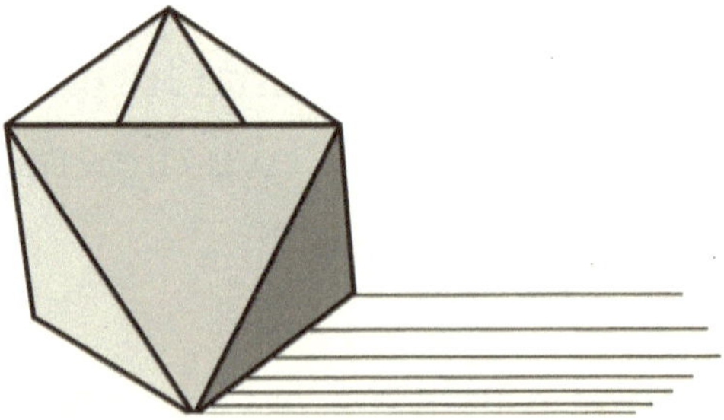

My second original origami design, this open antiprism and the tetrahedron based on this design, prompted me to learn how to diagram origami.

The design began as an attempt to twist a sheet of paper into an efficient box.

While elegant in this final form, getting here was messy. Hours of folding and unfolding resulted in a twisted mess. Additional hours of reverse engineering resulted in this refined design.

Starting with an equilateral triangle, the first stage of this design divides the main triangle into four groups of four equilateral triangles.

The second stage consists of twisting the three corners into the middle, folding the ends over to lock the design into shape.

A third stage, illustrated in the next diagram, provides a new approach to forming a tetrahedron.

01 | Tetrahedron from Triangular Open Antiprism

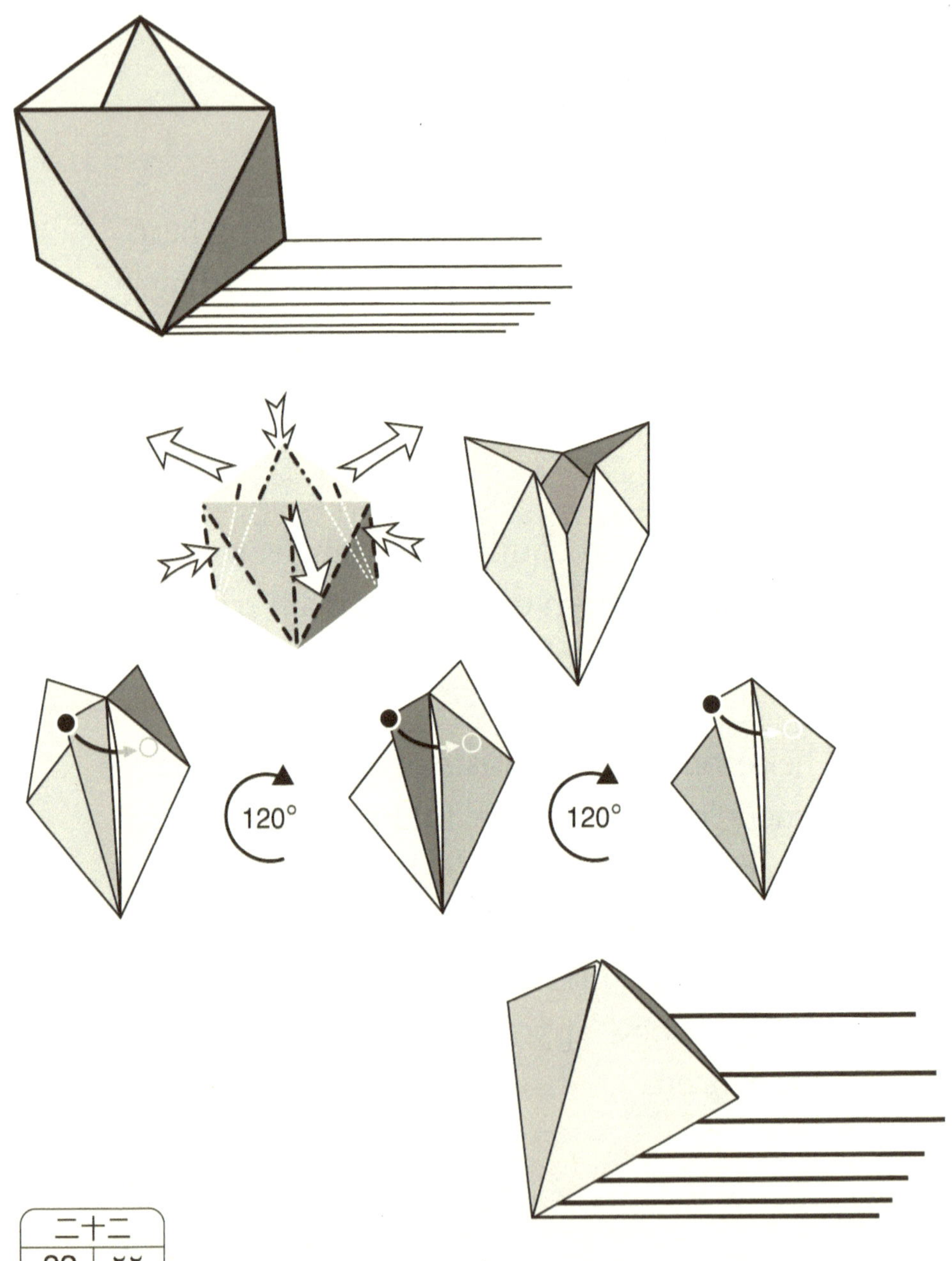

As I initially experimented with this design, the technique amounted to squishing and twisting a sheet of paper into a roughly pyramid shaped box. While the start looked more like foil wrapping a chocolate candy, after a few hours there seemed to be some form to the fabric. What took the most time was reverse engineering the stumbled-upon structure. Repeatability requires clear documentation, which ideally begins with a clear and detailed understanding. Once I figured how I did what, the first step was doing it again a few times. A proper diagram seemed appropriate after multiple individuals well accomplished in the origami community concurred this design was in fact one they had not seen before. Publishing this original design would require me to learn to diagram.

The triangular sides of the present antiprism alternate, one pointing up and the next pointing down. Those three pointing down have long sides at the top, at the open end of the form. Closing this open end is accomplished by folding these three sides outward to form tabs. These tabs may then be tucked in to adjacent slots to finish the tetrahedron.

02 | Octahedron Box from Open Triangular Antiprism

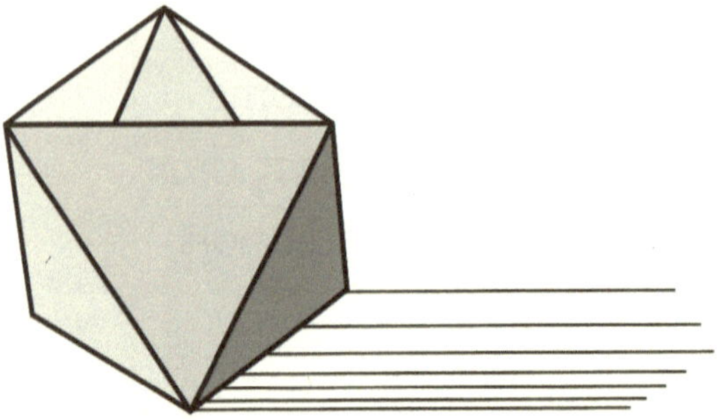

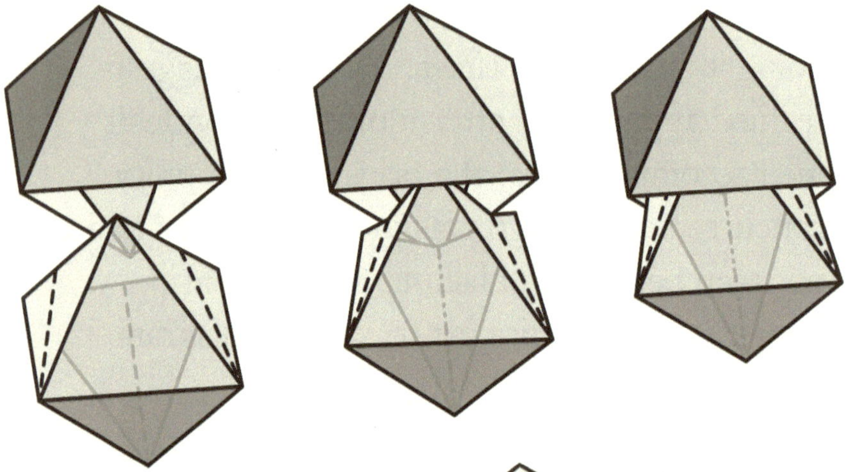

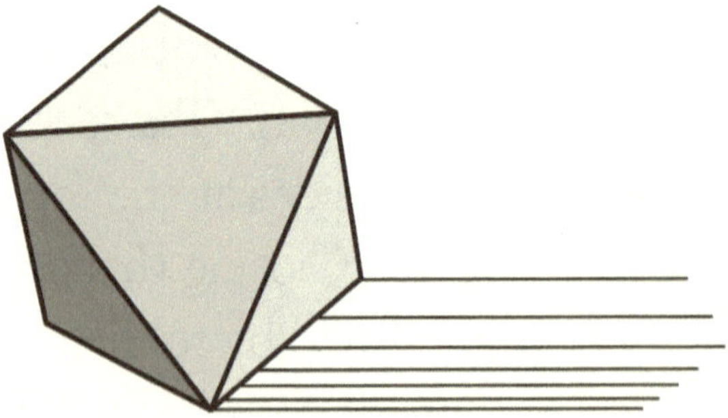

While the tetrahedron design can be used as a closed box, here is another approach.

Nesting one open triangular antiprism inside another at first glance is obvious, just like any other box. Right? Kinda.

The geometry of an antiprism is such that they don't nest cleanly. They are wider on one end where they are narrower on the other, and narrower on one end where they are wider on the other.

As the central figure in this diagram shows, the walls can be pushed in slightly and the one half pushed into the other. Once nested, the inner half opens up again, locking into the outer half.

This process, illustrated here with two open triangular antiprisms, can in fact be applied to a pair of any type of open antiprisms.

08 | Tetrahedron Box with Lid

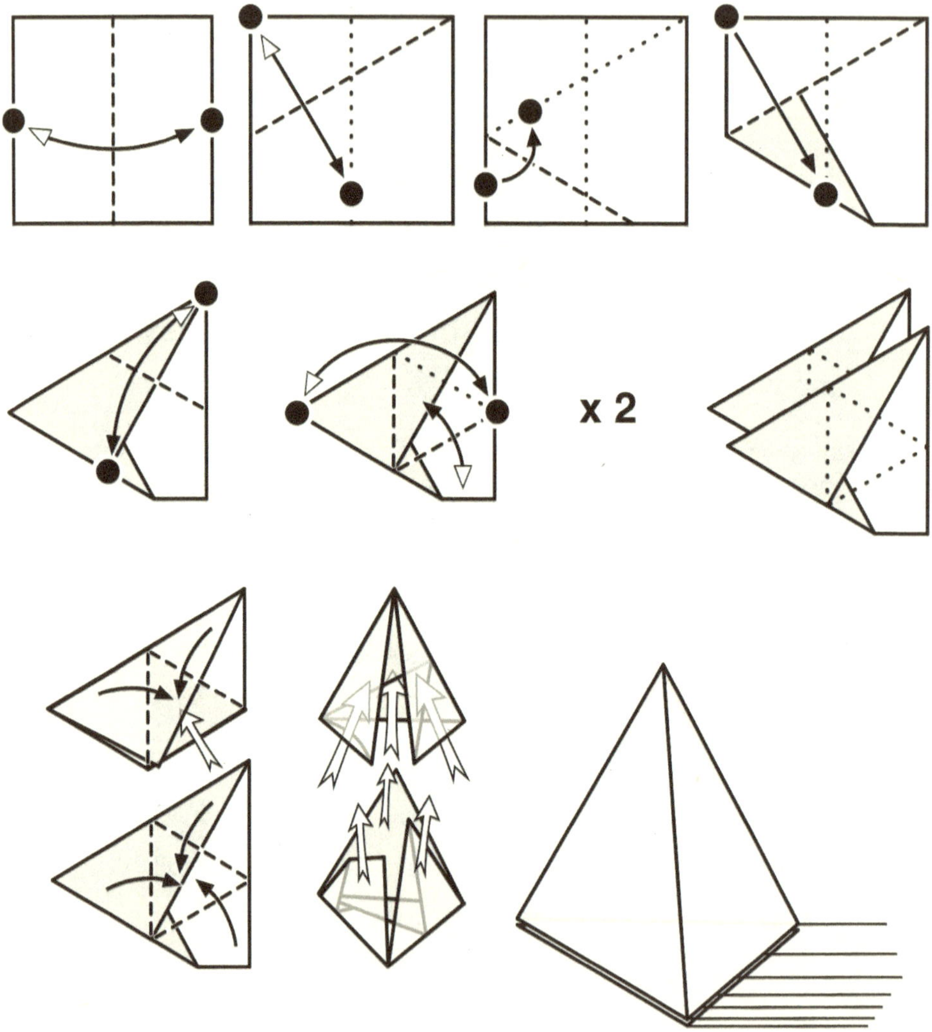

x 2

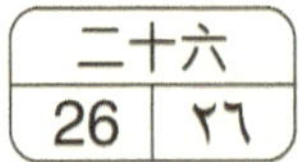

Here's a fun and relatively easy box, great for packaging a gift, or simply as a decoration.

Other box designs presented here will show two identical parts, open prisms or open antiprisms, with the open ends nested one into the other.

This box takes a slightly modified approach. Two identical parts are folded, triangles folded into triangles. One is formed into a box, with the three points folded up and together. The second is folded into itself, forming a set of three connected pockets, into which slide the three sides of the first part.

One of the edges is open, and can be used as the mouth of a puppet, or as a coin slot as in a piggy bank.

Enclosing one of these complete boxes in a second complete box, offset so the open edges don't overlap, forms a securely enclosed package.

16 | Common Box Corners

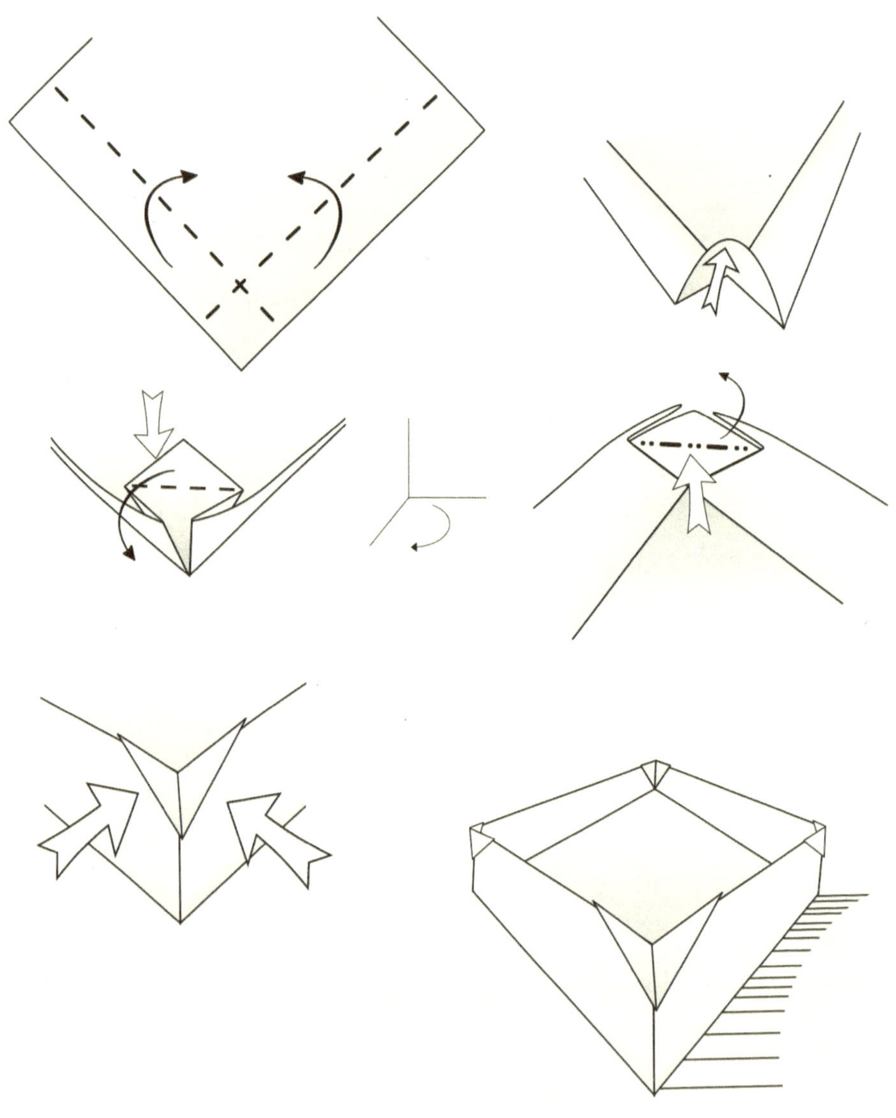

Presented is my original diagram of this standard origami design, the corner of a common box.

Pleats move the extra material out of the way so the side walls can be folded up, perpendicular to their original position. As the corner of the paper extends above the edge of the upright walls, there is room to fold that down over the corner. This fold is then bisected by the fold squaring the upright edge of the corner. The intersection of folds is a useful tool to prevent a design from unfolding.

This is the standard method for folding a square or rectangular open prism, where the 90 degree corners of the bottom are aligned with the 90 degree corners of the top.

New approaches to the corners of open prisms and open antiprisms are explored in the next few designs.

17 | Hexagon Open Antiprism

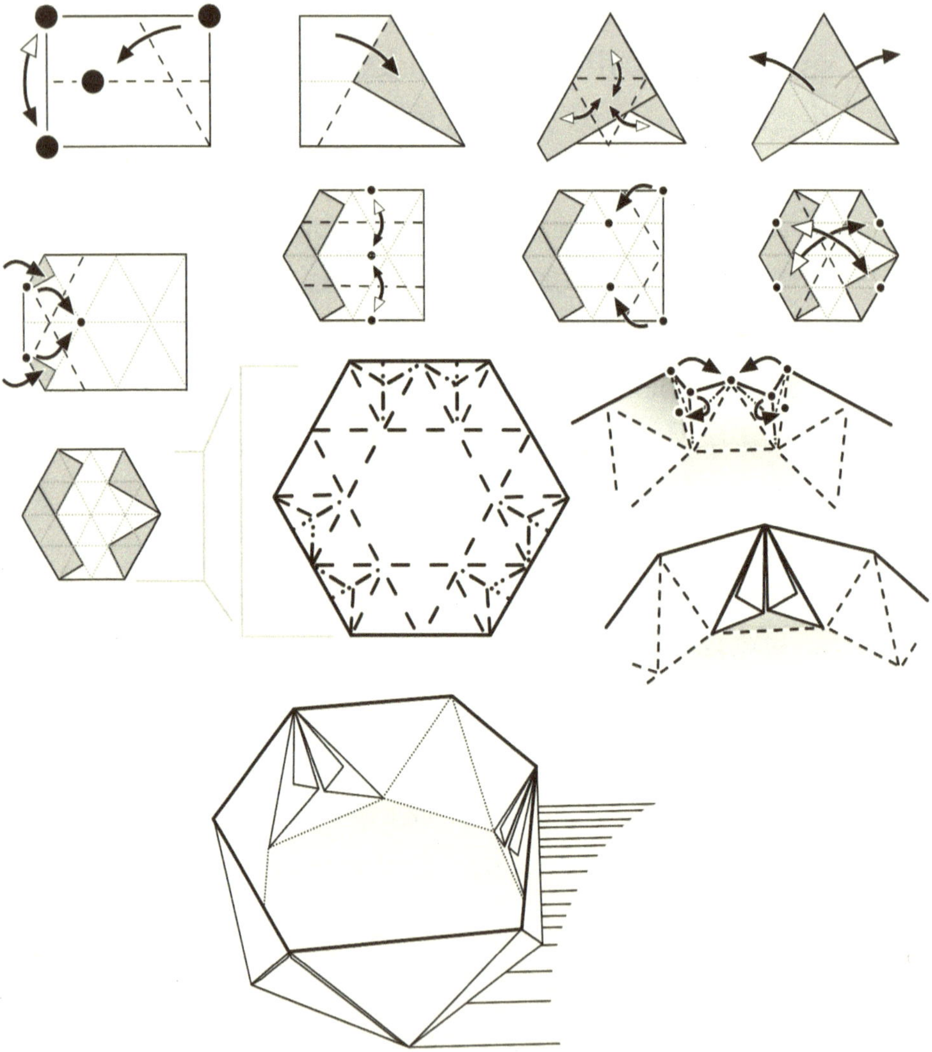

Folding a hexagonal antiprism starts with a hexagon.

Folding a hexagon starts with... a triangle.

Hexagons are extremely common in nature, and yet seem to carry a feeling of modern and unusual design.

The first half of this diagram presents steps folding a rectangular sheet of paper. Generally 4:3 in proportion, this would include common Letter and A4 size paper.

The folds establish a triangular pattern of creases that are the basis for a hexagon.

Starting from a regular hexagon is also possible, which would mean starting half way through the diagram.

Zooming in on the hexagon, the remaining folds are shown, mostly along established crease lines.

Only the locking folds of the corner pleats make new creases.

18 | Triangle Open Prism

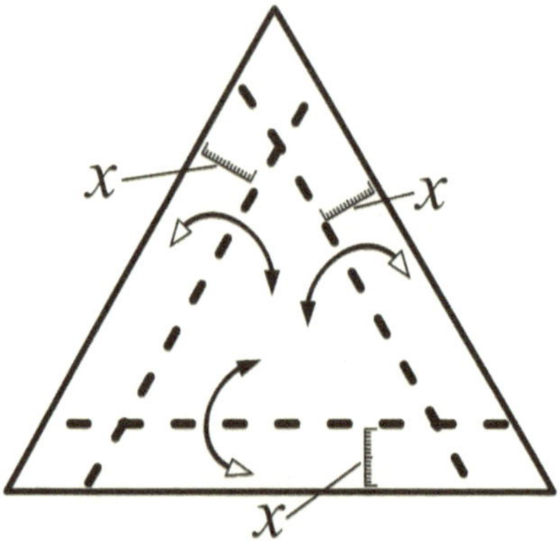

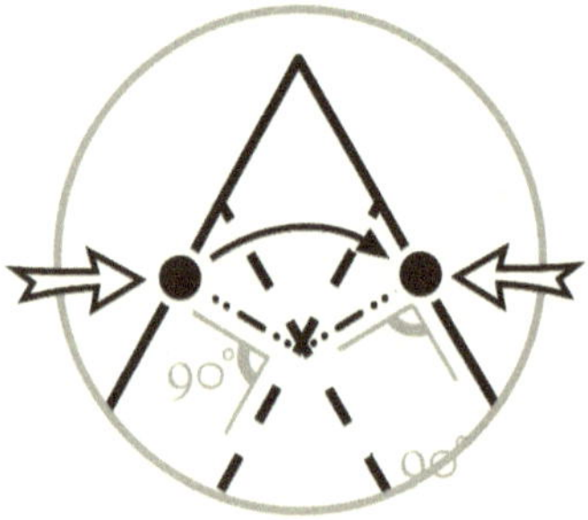

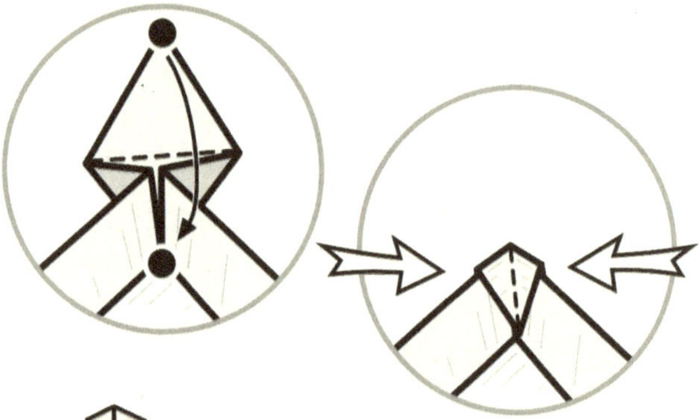

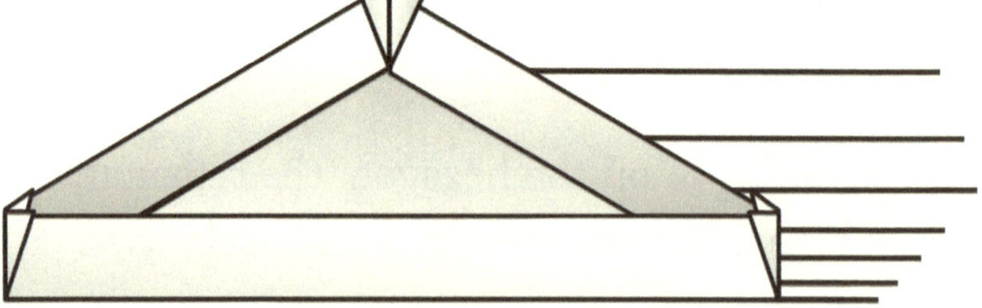

In this design, the corners of a common box are adapted to a triangular open prism. Flexibility to create different sized and proportioned pieces motivated this design and others like it in this collection.

The "x" in the diagram is intended to show that each of the edge sections are of the same width. This means the perpendicular walls of the finished tray will all be of the same height. Each corner is folded the same way, so only one corner is detailed in three circular insets.

In the first circle, the corner is formed by bringing the two large dots together. The curved arrow shows one large dot being folded to meet the other. The large outlined arrows show how the paper is to be pushed, or pinched together in this step.

The middle circle shows the resulting tab that is folded in and down, once again using an arrow with two large dots showing points that are being brought together.

Finally in the third circle the corner is shown being pinched together into shape.

19 | Open Prism from Truncated Triangle

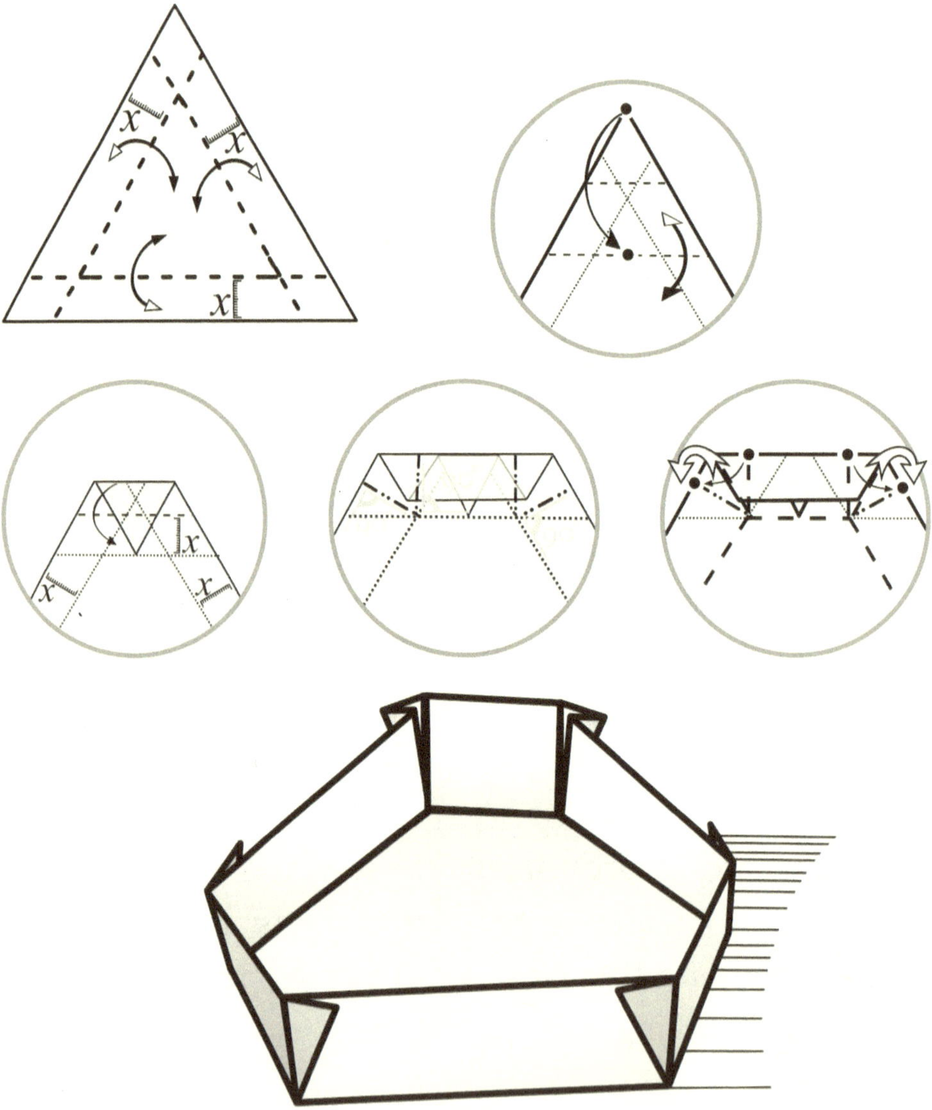

Truncated shapes have their corners cut off. In the case of this design, an open prism is formed from a three sided triangle modified to a six sided hexagon with short sides where the triangle's points would otherwise be.

In the first figure, top left, an equilateral triangle shaped piece of paper is shown. This could be a sheet of paper cut to this shape, or it may be a triangle folded from a sheet of paper.

An equal distance is marked off on each side, with a fold made parallel to each side.
A given amount is folded down equally at each corner. One corner, enlarged, is shown in the circular insets of the second row. The paper is folded down along this small side so the small sides have folds parallel at the same distance from the edge as the larger sides.
In the middle circular inset, mountain folds are made at the corners at 90 degrees, perpendicular to the edges. The final circular inset shows pleats being pushed out as the corners of the finished piece are formed. Note the black dots being brought together at each corner.

21 | Pentagon Open Antiprism from Regular Pentagon

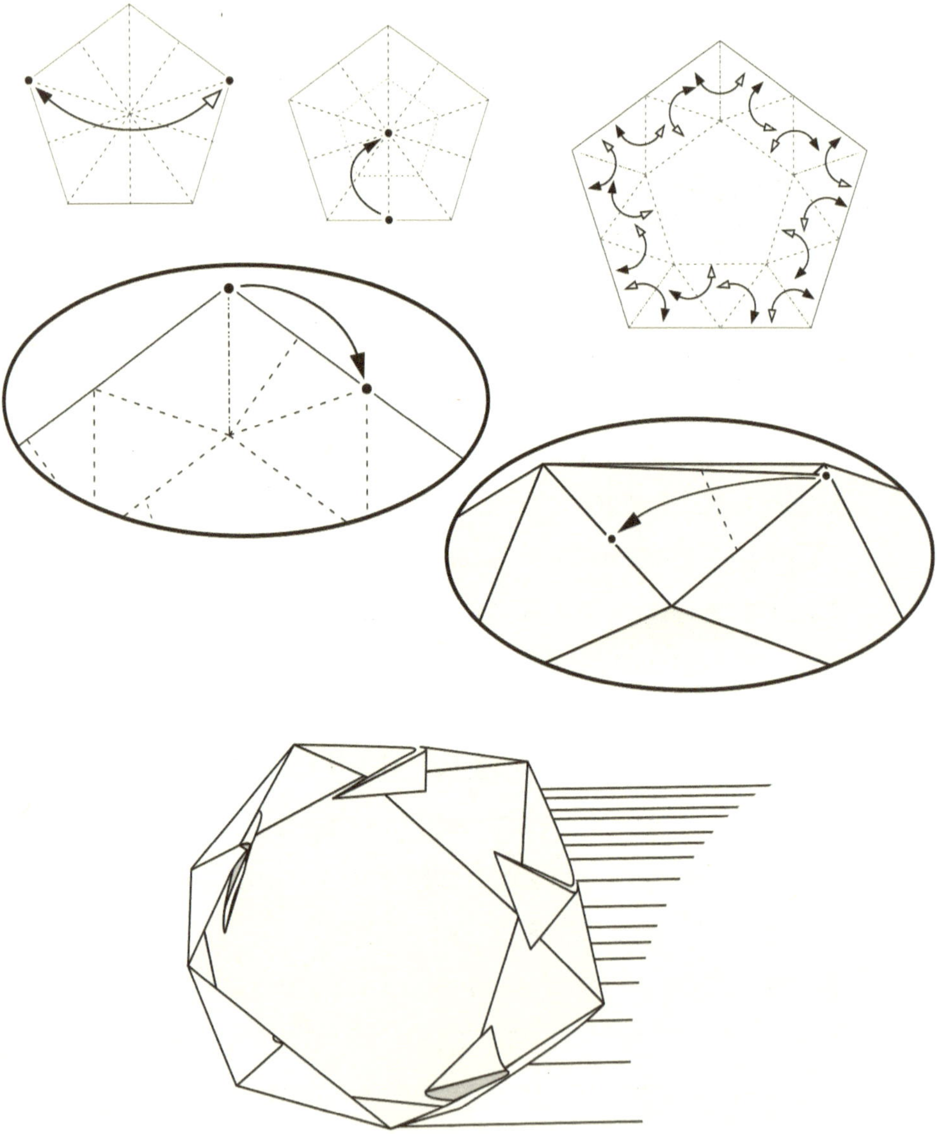

Open antiprisms like this can be made into a box, one nested and locked into a second.

The first figure shows one fold being made. That fold is then unfolded leaving a crease. This is repeated at other points, resulting in the set of creases shown.
The second figure shows only one fold. This is repeated with each side. These creases should only be sharply defined between the radial creases as illustrated.
The third figure shows all the folds and unfolds around the edges of the paper. These define a series of equilateral triangles.
Each point, with one point zoomed in and illustrated in the two oval insets, is folded to one side forming a pleat. The second oval inset shows that pleat being folded perpendicular to the fold with which it is formed. This locks the pleat somewhat, making it less likely to unfold.

After every point has a pleat folded, the finished open antiprism appears as illustrated.

22 | Truncated Triangle Open Antiprism from Rectangle

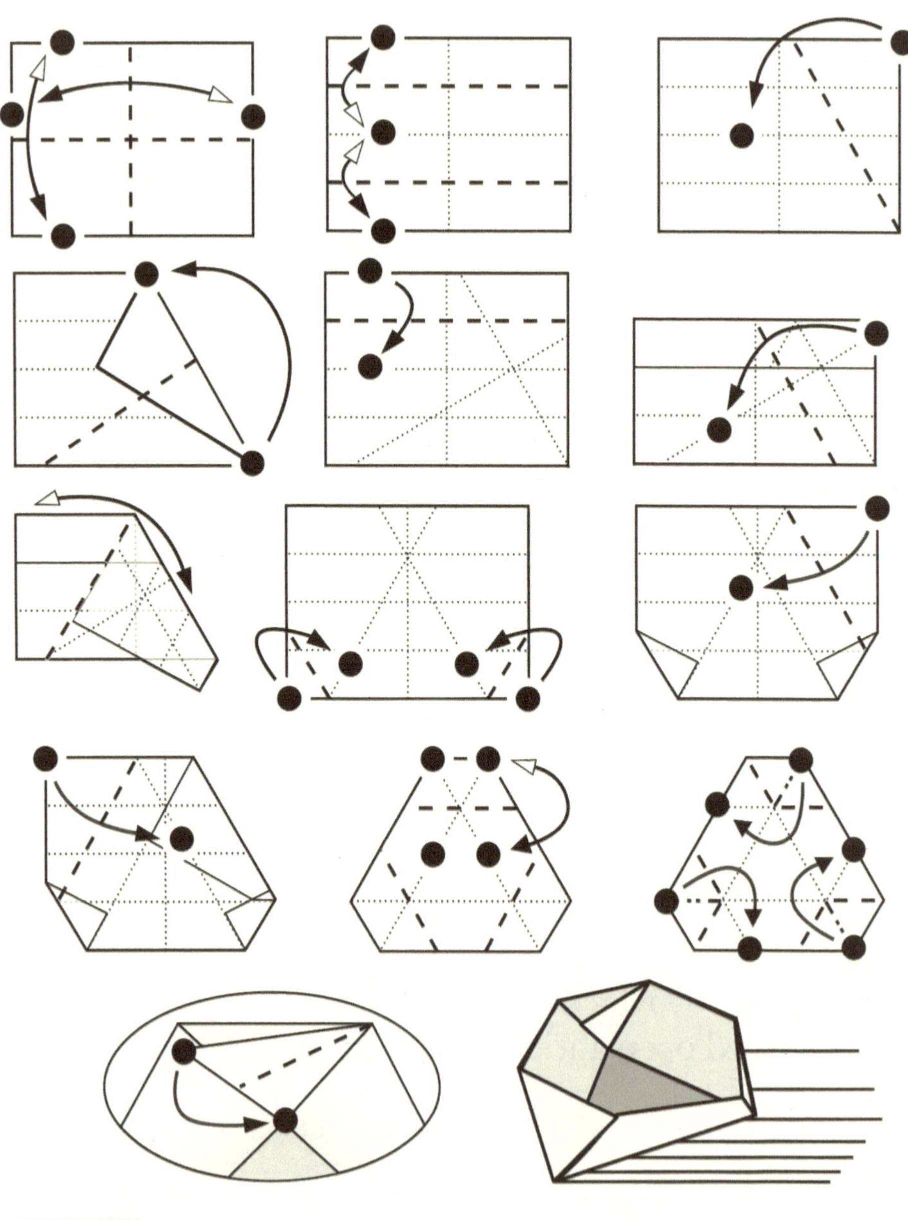

It is important that this design is centered on the rectangular paper. Once the first side of the large equilateral triangle is formed, that fold is bisected with a perpendicular fold. The first side of the large equilateral triangle may then be shifted along that crease. In this instance, in figure six, the triangle meets the center line at the top of the paper.

In figure eight the bottom corners are folded up along the creases forming the central triangle's sides. The upper large dots sit on those creases. In figure nine the top edge corners are likewise folded down and in as illustrated.

Next we see four large dots, where the top edge corners are folded down to points along the established creases, with this fold intersecting the crossing of the two creases. This is to be repeated with the other two shorter sides.

Lastly, three pleats are folded, one at each short side. The oval inset shows one pleat being folded down to prevent the design unfolding. This is to be repeated on each of the three pleats.

23 | Geodesic Dome Open Icosahedron from Rectangle

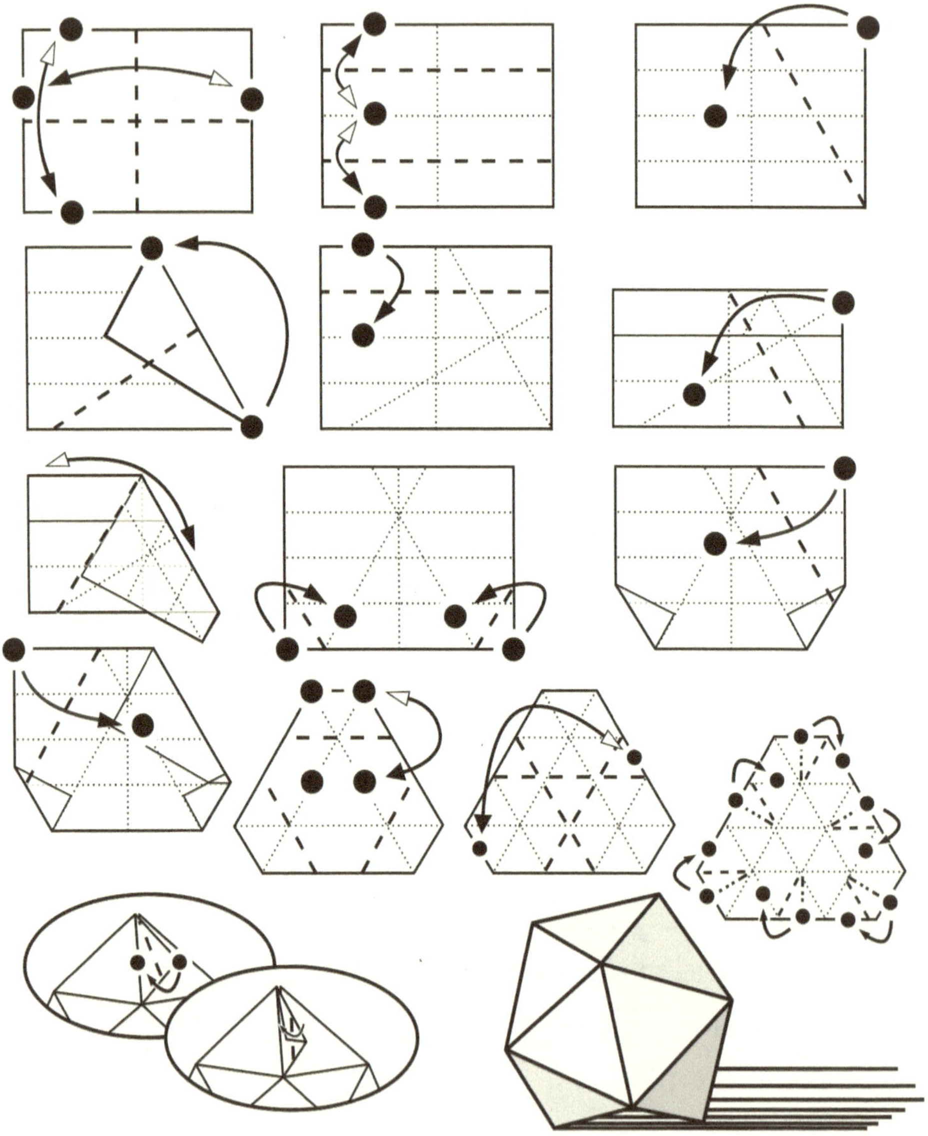

THE NEXT TWO DESIGNS, NUMBERED 23 AND 28, ARE DESCRIBED TOGETHER IN THE ACCOMPANYING TWO PAGES.

Buckminster Fuller designed maps, cars, houses and was a celebrated artist and engineer.

From the text of one of his patents:

"A good index to the performance of any building frame is the structural weight required to shelter a square foot of floor from the weather. In conventional wall and roof designs the figure is often 50 pounds to the square foot. I have discovered how to do the job at around 0.78 pounds per square foot by constructing a frame of generally spherical form in which the main structural elements are interconnected in a geodesic pattern of approximate great circle arcs intersecting to form a three-way grid, and covering or lining this frame with a skin of plastic material."

"Geodesic ⟦is defined as⟧ of or pertaining to great circles of a sphere, or of arcs of such circles; as a geodesic line, hence a line which is a great circle or arc thereof; and

28 | Geodesic Dome Open Icosahedron from Square

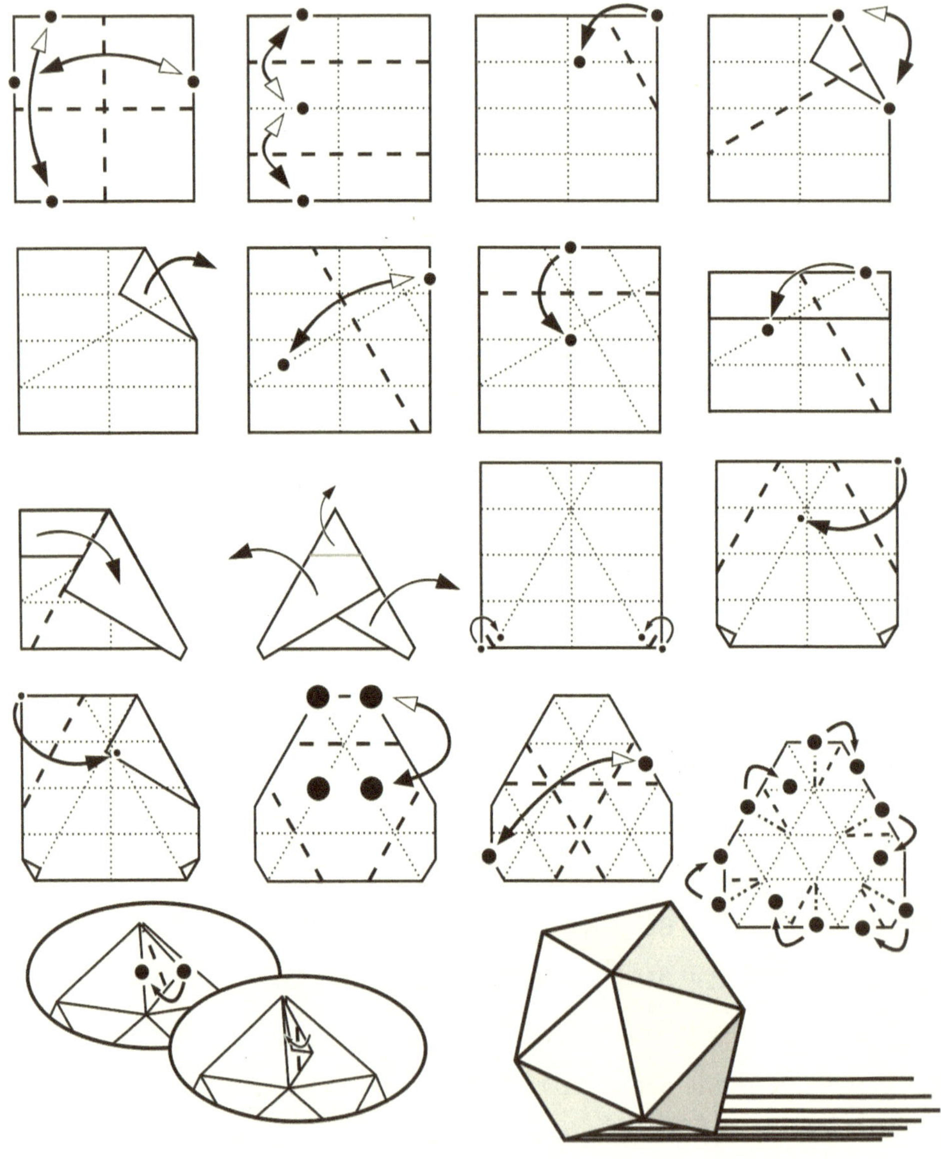

as a geodesic pattern, hence a pattern created by the intersections of great circle lines or arcs, or their chords."

"In my preferred construction, the grids are formed on the faces of a spherical icosahedron."

(United States patent 2,682,235 for Building Construction filed in 1951)

The regular icosahedron is a 20 sided Platonic Solid, a fundamental form in geometry.

This origami design results in an open regular icosahedron, open as it is missing four of the twenty regular triangle panels on one side.

Similar to the open antiprisms presented in this collection, two of these open icosahedrons may be nested so as to form a box like form, a complete closed icosahedron.

Guidance from the previous design, numbered 22, may be helpful in understanding the reference dots and arrows used in these diagrams.

26 | Open Anticube
Square Antiprism

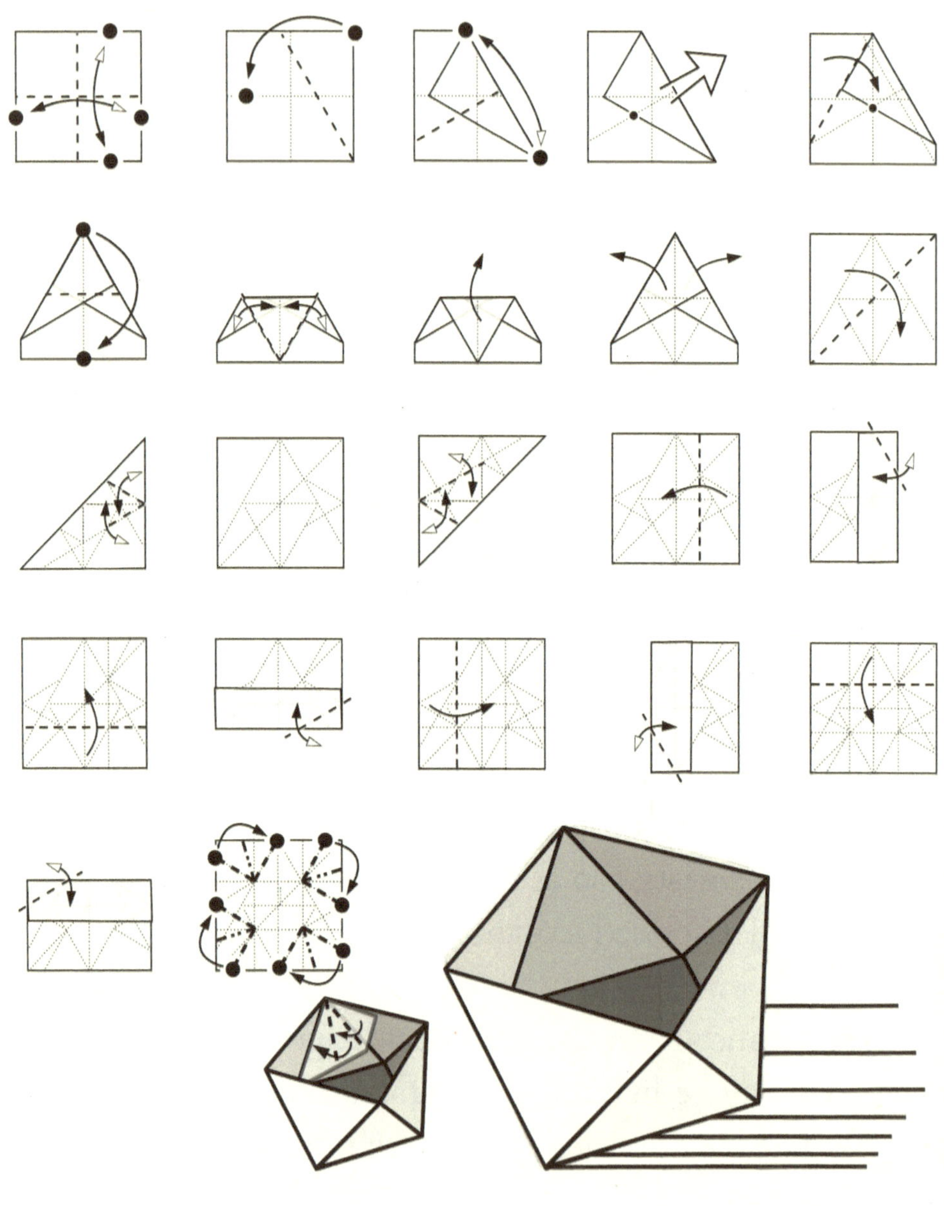

In the interest of being complete, it seemed appropriate to design and document the folding of a variety of regular open antiprisms.

This diagram documents my design for an open antiprism based on a square.

Another name for a square regular antiprism is an anticube. Perhaps obvious at this point, the regular square prism would be a cube.

This open antiprism, like other antiprisms, may nest one inside another to make a box.

This diagram provides a detailed progression of folds that build one upon the other. Perhaps the ideal would be folding one sheet of paper as diagrammed, and then tracing only the necessary lines onto a second sheet. These essential lines may then be scored and folded with all panels clean of unnecessary folds.

In the next to last figure, the tiny folds inside the form are shown. These lock the form by adding two intersecting folds to otherwise loose flaps.

31 | Triaugmented Triangular Open Prism from Square

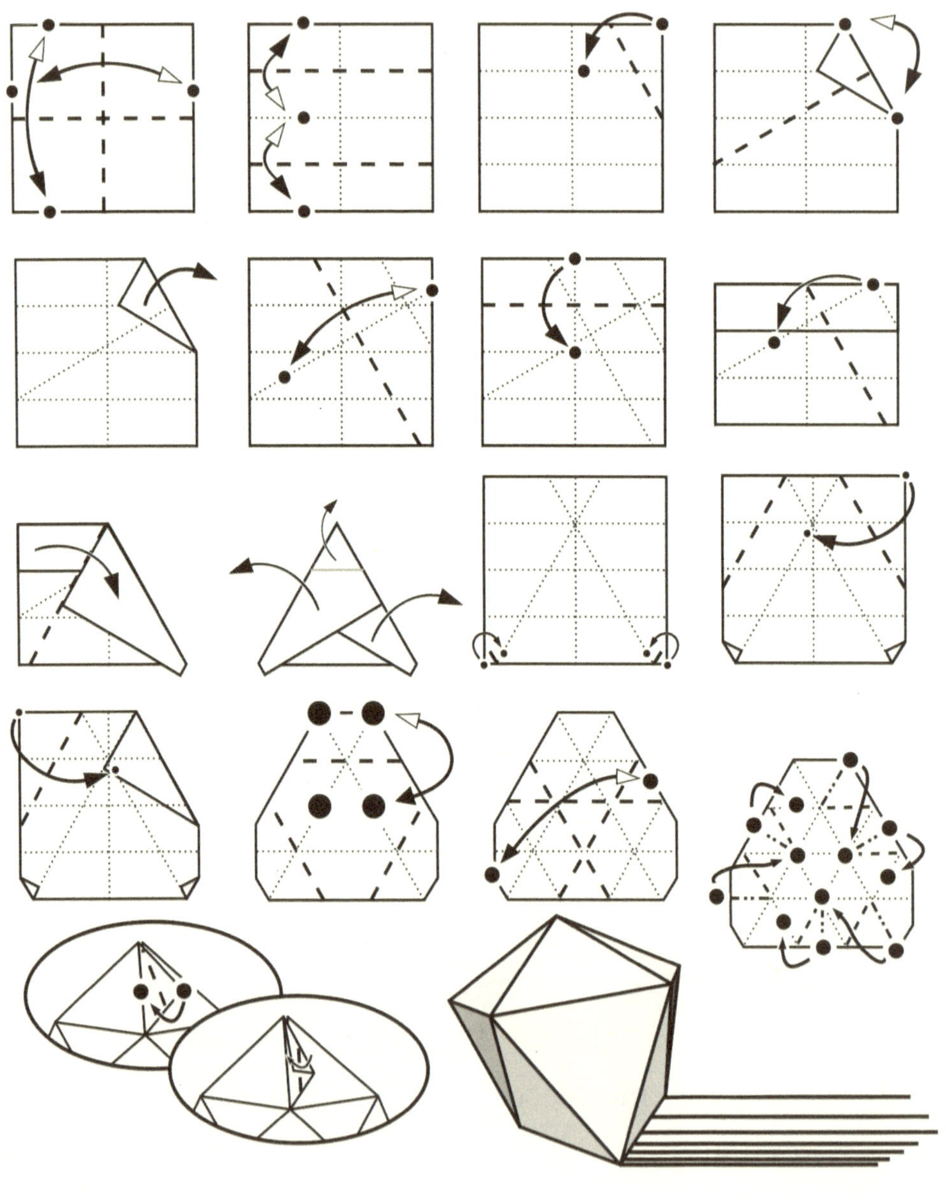

Here is an example of an augmented prism, where the side walls of the prism are themselves three dimensional forms.

In this instance a simple triangle based prism has three sides, each a square. From each of these square sides proceeds a square based pyramid each with four triangular sides. Each of the ends of the core prism and the walls of the protruding pyramids are the exact same sized regular triangle.

This shape made an appearance while I was playing with folding the middle steps in different ways, seeing what different configurations looked like. This had interesting symmetry and searching through various geometry examples I found and learned more about the significance of this form.

Looking at this from different angles reveals both symmetry and asymmetry. The symmetry disappears from view completely at times.

42 | Two Part Cube
Ho Tsak-man, Haruo Hosoya

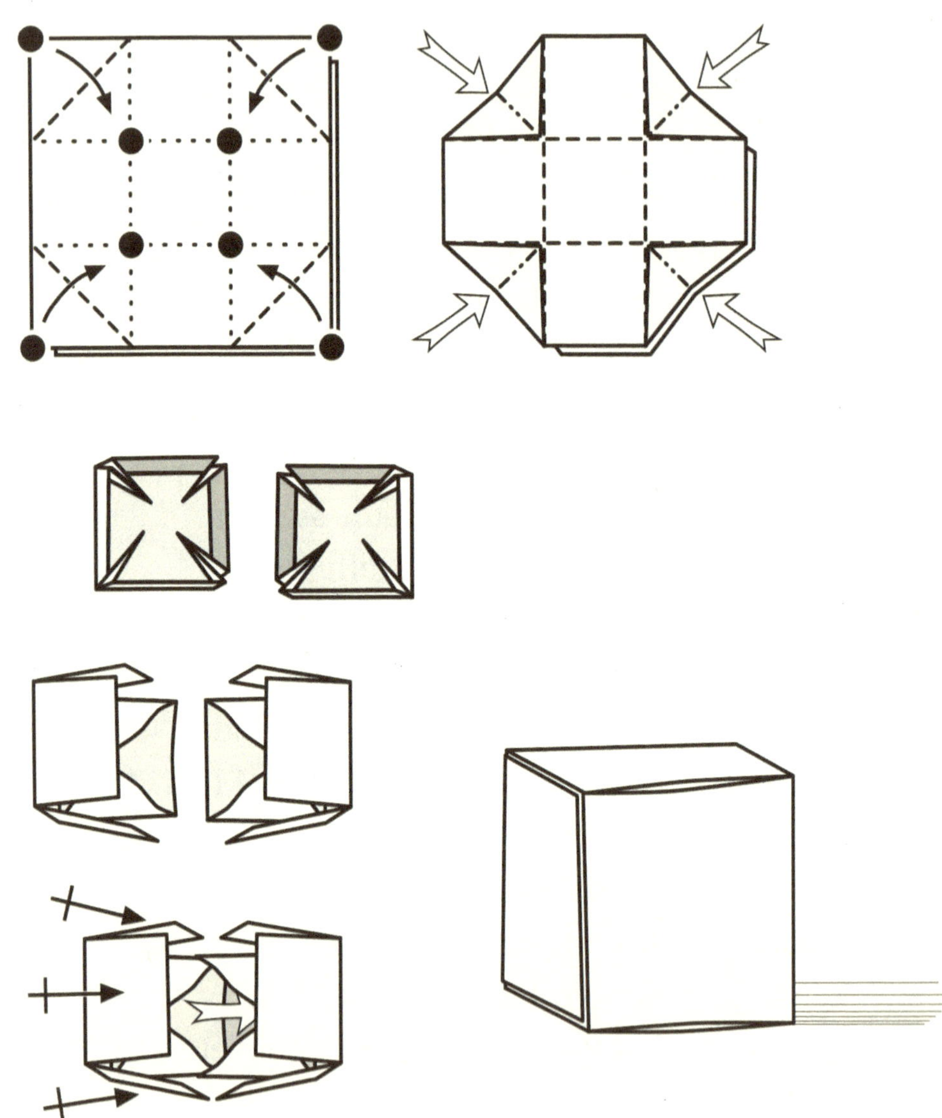

Designs are sometimes developed independently by multiple people. This design was first published by Ho Tsak-man in The Flapping Bird, issue 20, 1974. Subsequently this was published by Haruo Hosoya in the 1985 book Origami for the Connoisseur by Kunihiko Kasahara and Toshie Takahama. Here is my original diagram for this design—one that I thought I invented.

Two identical square open prisms are formed with the corner pleats folded in half on a diagonal. The two parts nest one into the other forming a box from two halves. Assembling these two halves is more difficult than folding them. The stability of the structure is only established after the two parts are joined. Starting by joining the two halves on one side provides some initial stability. Individually inserting the corner pleats of the one half into the corner edges of the other is one way to build on that initial stability and fully join the two parts.

This diagram uses an arrow with a perpendicular line across one end to illustrate that the step shown is to be repeated once on each of the remaining three sides of the form. Detail of the three dimensional geometry of the forms is not fully diagrammed.

39 | Triangle Lock Box

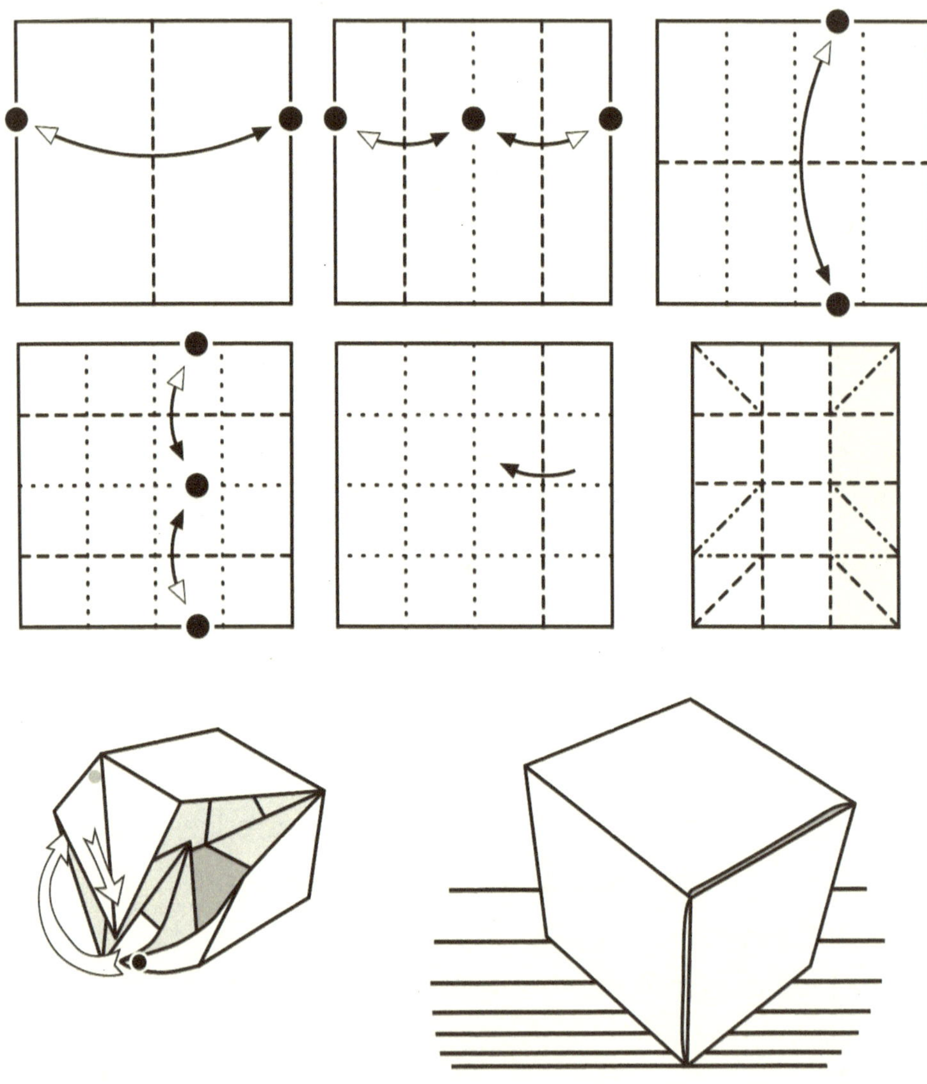

Minimalist in design, edges of the paper just touch to form one edge of the finished box.

Pleated sides lock the form together. Shown is the preferred arrangement, one that provides clean cube faces and a stable form.

In the first three figures, a square sheet of paper is folded in halves resulting in a four by four grid of squares.

Folding one side in, we arrive at the four by three square grid, the foundation of this design. A paper with proportions of 4:3 may be folded directly into this arrangement. Creases are fully shown in the sixth figure. Next all of the folds on one side are shown partially folded. The large dot in black is being folded to meet a second large dot. The gray color of this second dot indicates this point is inside the pleat, not directly visible. The point marked with the large black dot is tucked in, wrapping around the collection of side pleats and holding them all in place. The opposite side is illustrated in finished form for clarity. Leaving one tab out allows use of this form as a phone stand.

45 | Fast Maximal Open Cube

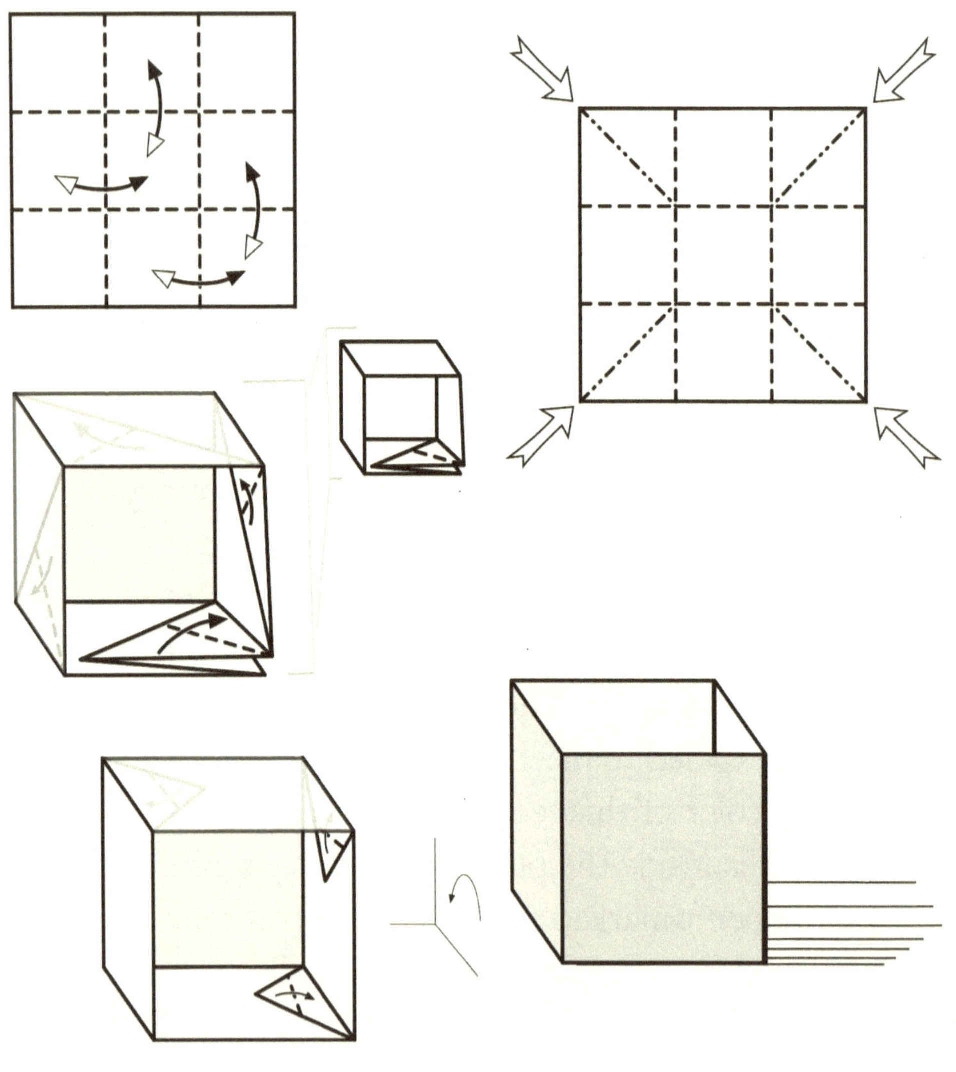

Many box designs exist, from simple to complex. Based on a simple set of folds, the corners of this box are locked with a slight twist.

Geometry—and I invite the reader to research this independently—proves the largest dimension possible will have edges one third the length of the edge of the starting square. This leads to a three by three grid, common among origami box designs.

With the goal of clean outside surfaces, my thinking looked back on my earlier designs. Some of these included corner pleats that were folded back on themselves, with perpendicular folds locking each other in place. Folding starts with a three square by three square grid. Each corner square is folded in, bringing up the sides of the cube. Multiple perpendicular folds stabilize the corner pleats, though they are not fixed to the inside surface of the cube.

This inefficient arrangement provides for extremely clean outside surfaces and a mechanically stable structure—an effective design overall.

46 | Dollar Bill Hinged Box

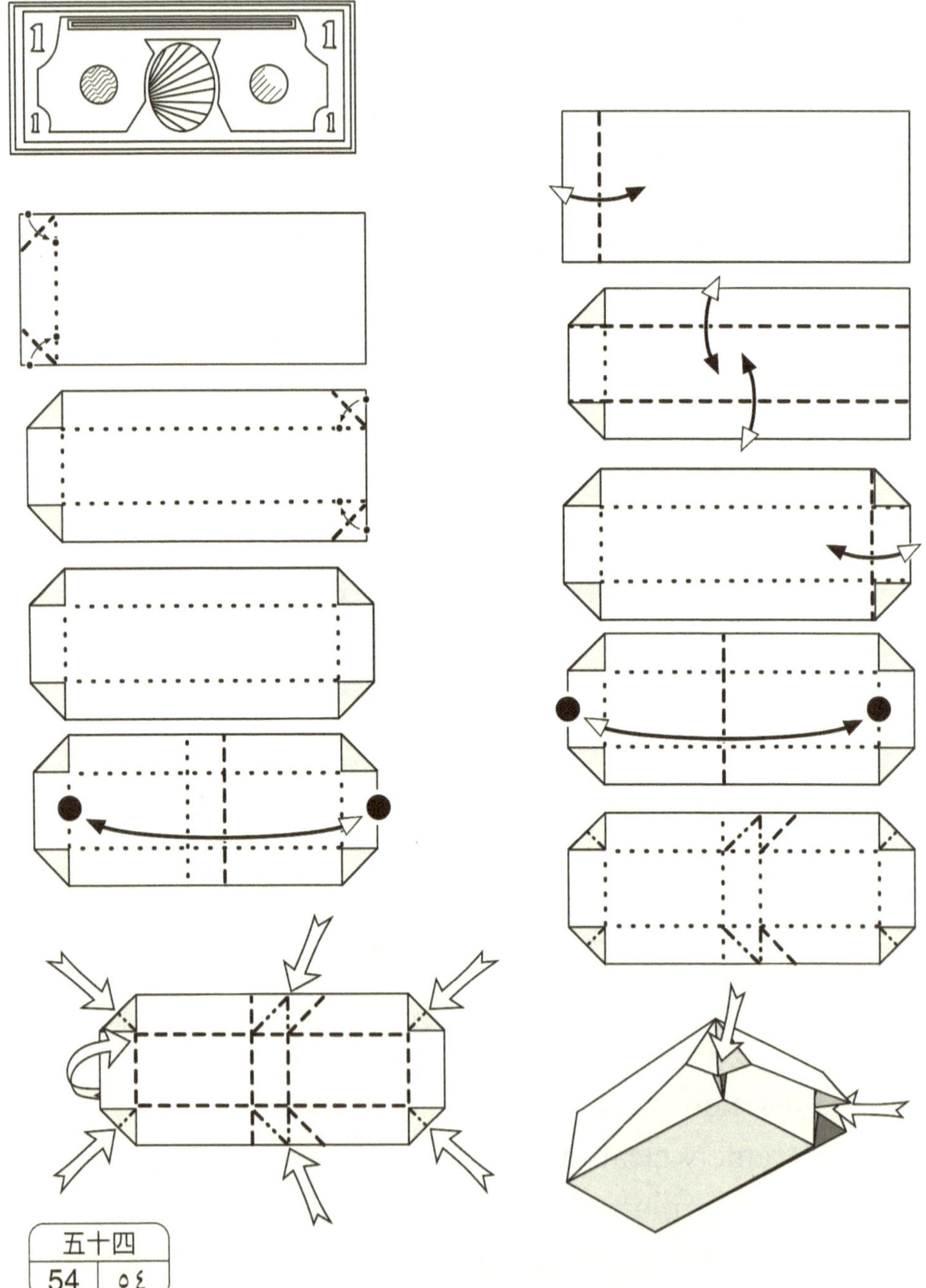

Dollar bills are ubiquitous pieces of paper that add intrinsic value to the novelty of an origami piece. Many designs exist specifically tailored to the dollar bill. Giving a gift wrapped in a bank note lends immediate visual impact. Opportunities for humor appear—like giving someone an empty box... folded from a hundred dollar bill.

So, here's the walk through. The flow here is from the top down, side to side, side to side, down to the bottom of the page.

First, the end of the bill is folded in and out. The corners on that end are then folded in to the first fold.

Those corners then define the height of the top and bottom edge folds and the folds of the far end.

Folding the far end of the paper to the near end's fold, and repeating for the other end, defines the hinge end of the box.

The final set of folds prepares the box to be folded in on itself, with all of the corners neatly tucking away.

48 | Hinged Box 2

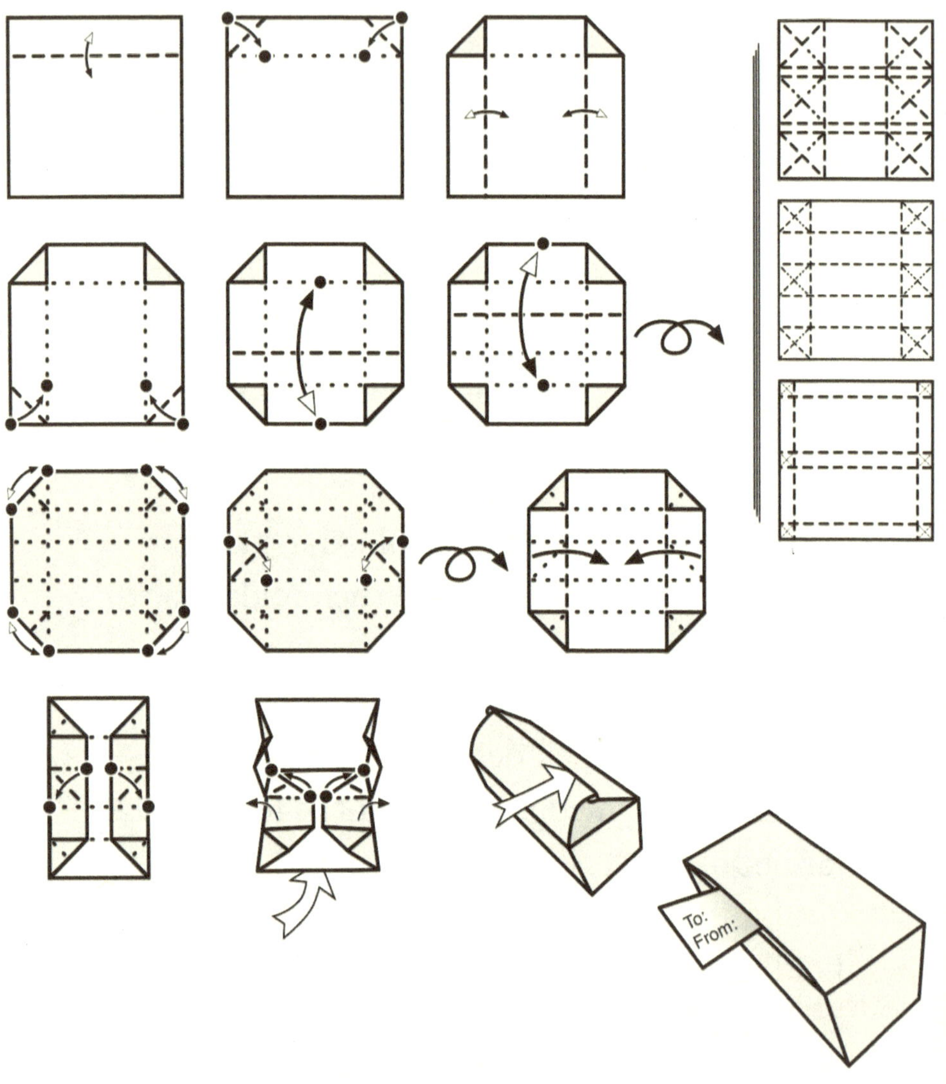

Following on the Dollar Bill Hinged Box design, a range of box sizes may be folded from any size paper. Applicable to paper of any proportion, square paper is illustrated. Corners of differing size and relative face sizes are illustrated as an aside on the right.

From flat, the paper is guided into three dimensions, stable only when completed. Visualizing the folding sequence that forms and closes the box was challenging.

The last row of figures presents this process.

From the bottom left, the first figure shows the points that are brought together and both lift and open the top half of the box.

Next, the second figure shows specific points being brought together. Arrows indicate how the side panels fold out from the center as the bottom of the box is pulled up towards the top half.

Finishing the box, the flap from the bottom of the box slides into the matching face of the top of the box. A gift tag or card may be placed inside the pocket formed.

Phone Stands

Utility drove the development of these origami designs.

Initially, a minor variation of another design resulted in a small pyramid with a tab extending out from the base. This worked well, though limited in height. Also, a number of the required folds felt superfluous.

Experience with that initial phone stand led to modified and refined designs. A much taller design resulted from the same size paper and with minimal folding.

It would seem that any shape could be used to lean a phone against. Due to the light weight of these designs, the weight of anything leaned against them quickly pushes them away. My solution across these designs is the provision of a tab extended out, where the phone sits and anchors the structure.

03 | Pyramid Phone Stand from Equilateral Triangle

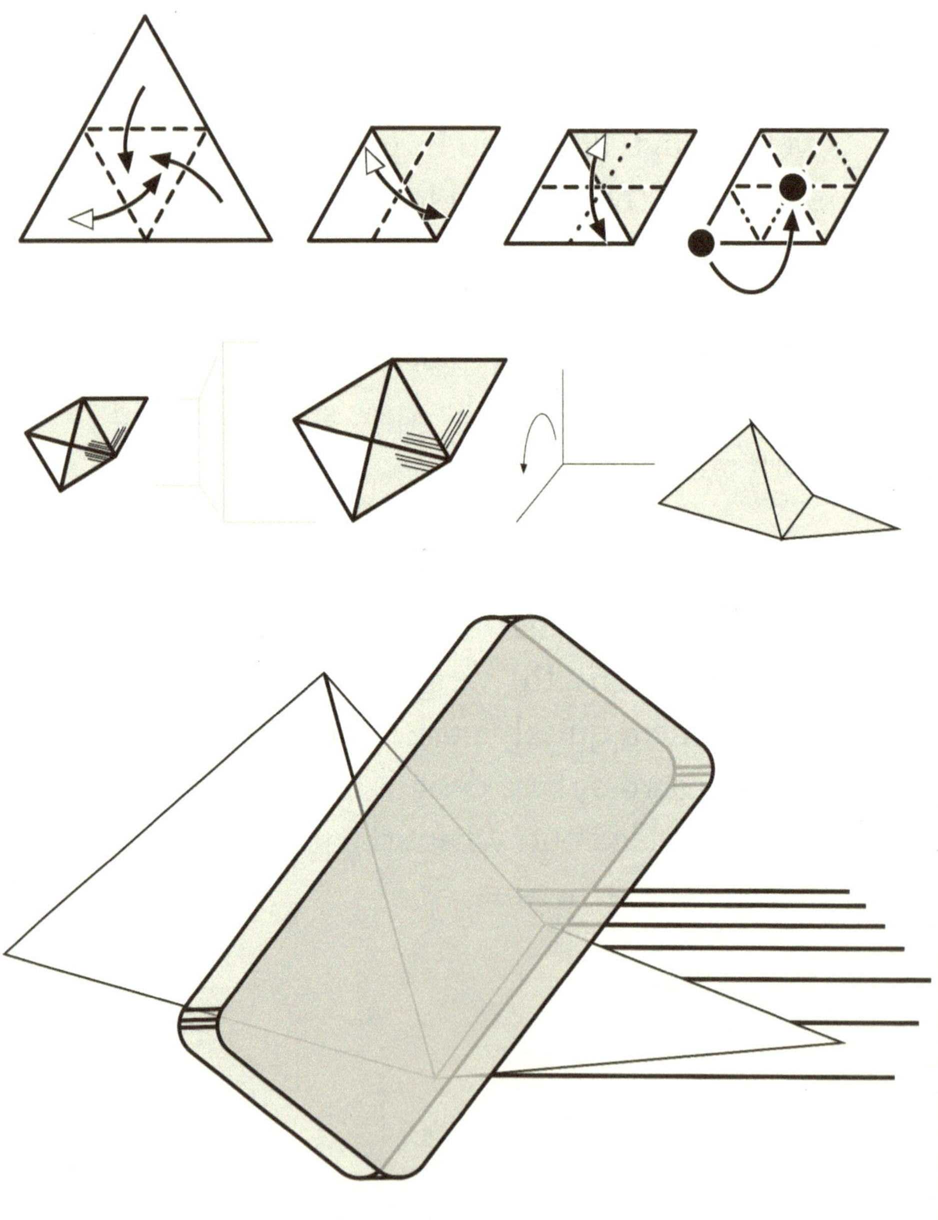

Folding triangles into triangles, this design ends with a twist that locks the form into place.

The present pyramid form is one of my early designs with only slight modification.

The middle row of figures resets the view, zooming in and then rotating the form on the Y/Z plane.

A tab is reserved out of the main pyramid for the phone to sit on. This anchors the system, so the weight of the phone does not push the stand away.

The height of this design limits the function, such that with a standard sheet of paper the resulting stand may only accommodate a phone laying on its side.

10 | Pyramid Phone Stand from Rectangle

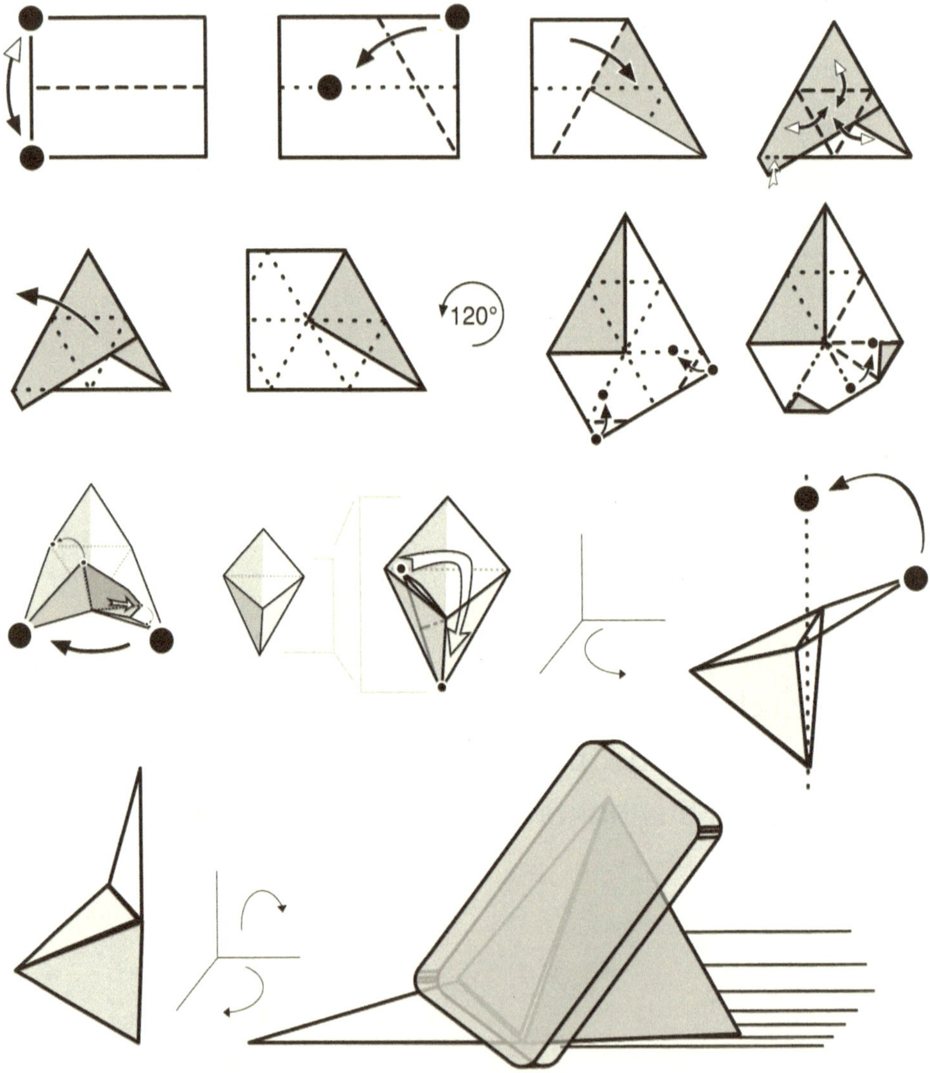

120°

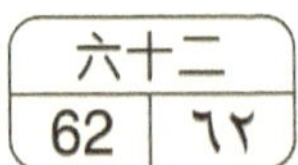

Starting with a rectangle, folding an equilateral triangle results in extra material available which this design utilizes.

After folding an equilateral triangle from a rectangle, it is partially unfolded.

The unfolded panel, already folded into triangle sections, is reincorporated and pushed in, locking the pyramid while leaving one corner of the original triangle unincorporated. This corner tab becomes the anchor the phone sits on, balancing the weight of the phone leaning against the pyramid.

The pyramid and the anchoring tab are both larger than the first phone stand design, relative to the size of the starting paper. This allows a phone to stand tall, in portrait orientation.

37 | Fast Phone Stand from Square

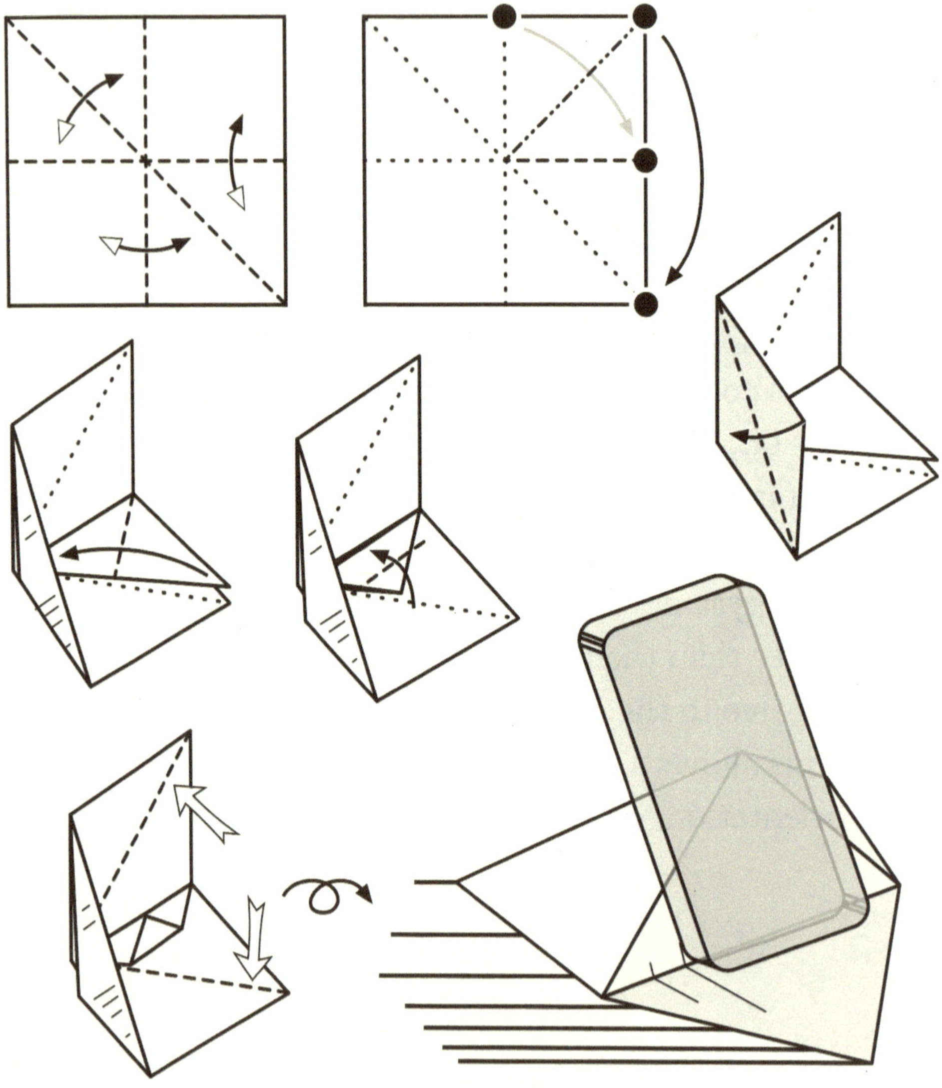

In this original origami design, I accomplish the goal of my previous phone stand designs using a square instead of a rectangle, and fewer folds.

Here is efficiency of time and materials, elegance of form and function.

In the third figure, the pleat is shown folded, and the adjacent panel is folded to make the tab on which the bottom of the phone will rest.

The last set of figures shows the pleat folded onto itself to keep it from unfolding.

While this has a large footprint and other imperfections, the design is highly optimized for speed of assembly and is effective for supporting any phone.

51 | Low Phone Stand

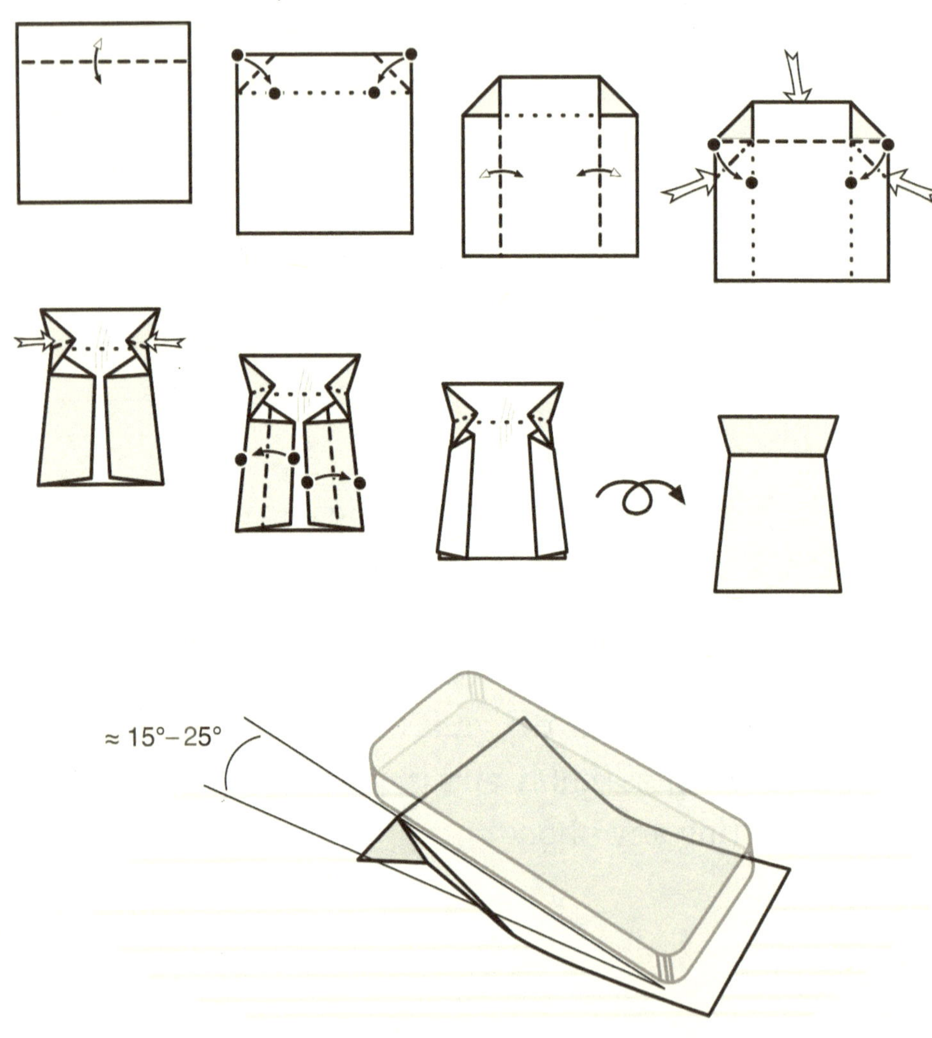

Ever needed a stand that held the phone at a convenient angle for hands free reading and typing? With origami, as long as you have a piece of paper, almost anything is easy to make with a few carefully placed folds.

This stand design holds the phone at a low angle, close to the table surface. Depending on the size of the paper and the relative sizes of the folds, the angle at which the top of the phone is lifted will change. The angle illustrated is in the 15 to 25 degree range.

Folds used in several other of my designs from envelopes to airplanes are combined in this design.

Minimal structure supports the phone, both in rise and also in preventing the phone from sliding down.

Structural strength is shifted by folds to the paper itself resisting tear or crush.

52 | Cord Connected Phone Stand

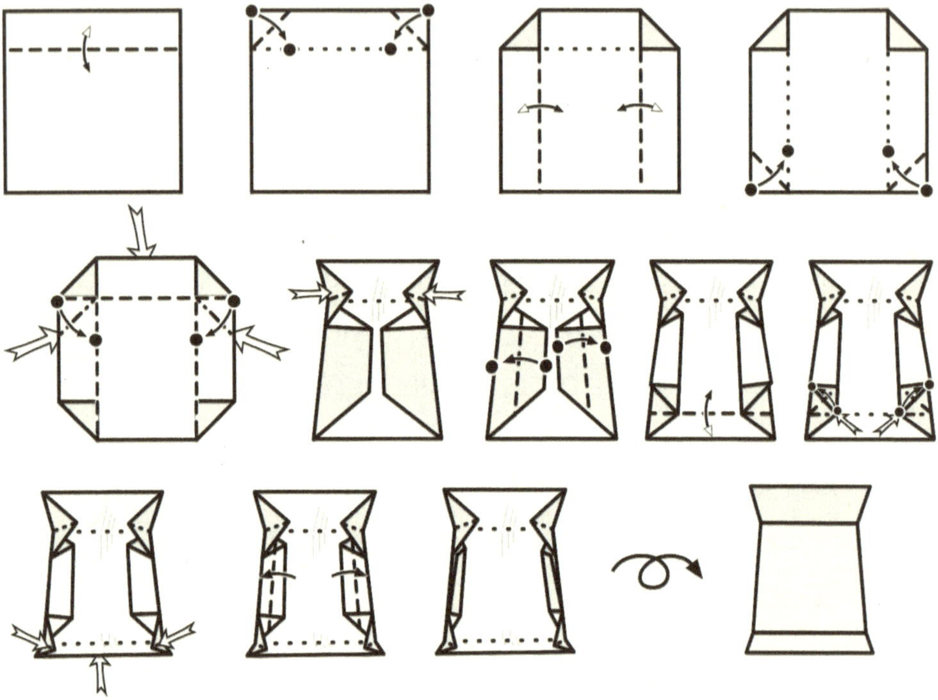

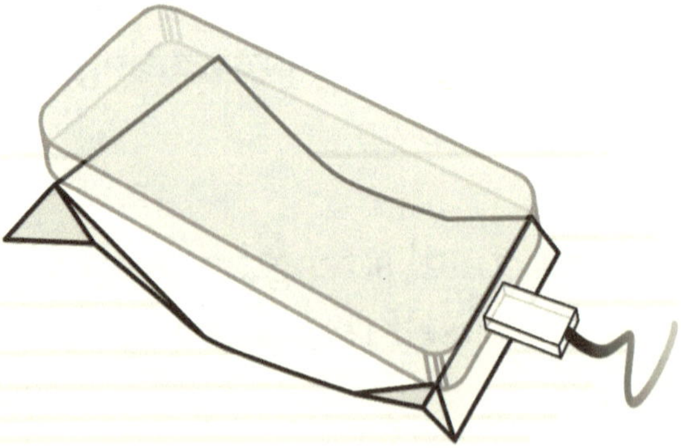

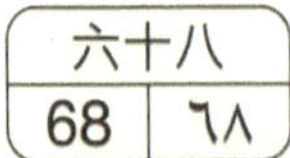

Resting a phone on a stand while connected requires providing space for the cord. This may be facilitated by setting the phone on a long edge, with the cord extending out to one side. This design provides a portrait or tall view of the screen while also making room for a cord.

First, the structure raises the top of the phone to make it easier to see the screen. Second, a similar structure raises the bottom of the phone to protect any attached wires.

While this is a complex three dimensional form, it readily folds flat when needed.

Origami is uniquely suited for storing a complex three dimensional form as a substantially flat structure requiring minimal input to convert to full three dimensional functionality. Stacking and nesting these forms may provide larger useful structures.

Basic Shapes

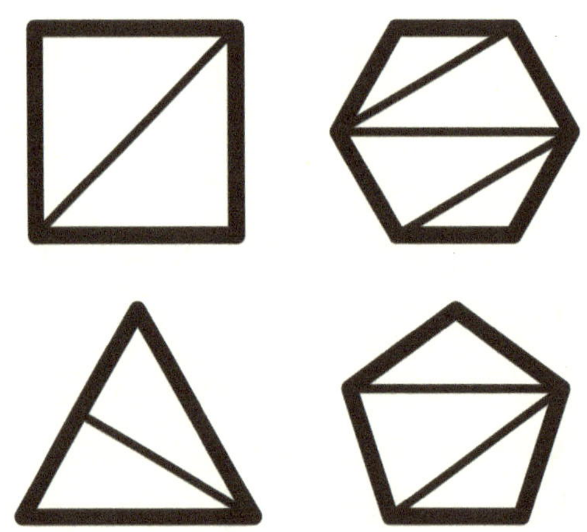

Triangles are integral to most of the designs presented in this collection. Even the cylinder design, which includes no triangular shape or fold, is directly built upon my various triangle based box and envelope designs.

Hexagons are interesting compound triangle forms. They are common in nature such as in the cells of a honeycomb or the shape of certain plants and crystals.

Regular uniform tiling of the Euclidean plane is only possible using equilateral triangles, squares and regular hexagons.

Tiling with hexagons minimizes the surface area between tiles, and so it is theorized that this efficiency of materials is why, for example, bees make their honeycombs using this shape.

Pentagons feel like an important shape, and have a clear connection to triangles.

These then are the basic shapes on which I focused. My work resulted in the following set of original origami designs and diagrams of these shapes.

04 | Hexagon from Equilateral Triangle

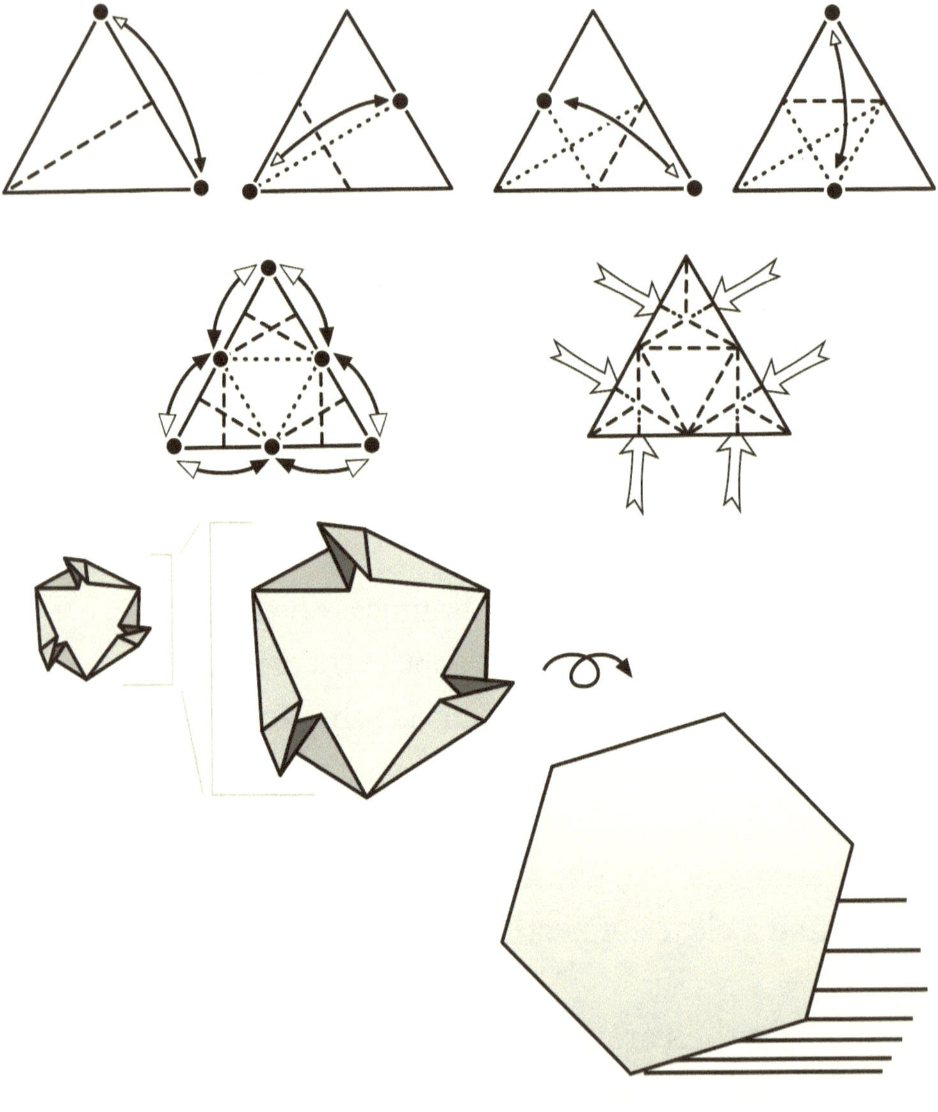

Here's a design that provides a quick and easy hexagon by pinching the points of an equilateral triangle and folding them down in a symmetrical fashion.

This ultimately provides a folded hexagon that may start with a rectangle, square or equilateral triangle. Further, this can continue to be folded into forms based on a hexagon.

Where a cut hexagon is required, this folded hexagon provides a clean and accurate method for making tracing and cutting templates.

The first figure in the second row illustrates the pleats needed to define the hexagon shape.

The second figure in that row shows the folds needed to bring the extra material back onto the hexagon.

Flipping the form over, one sees the finished form's clean side with no folds visible.

20 | Pentagon
Halves and Intersections

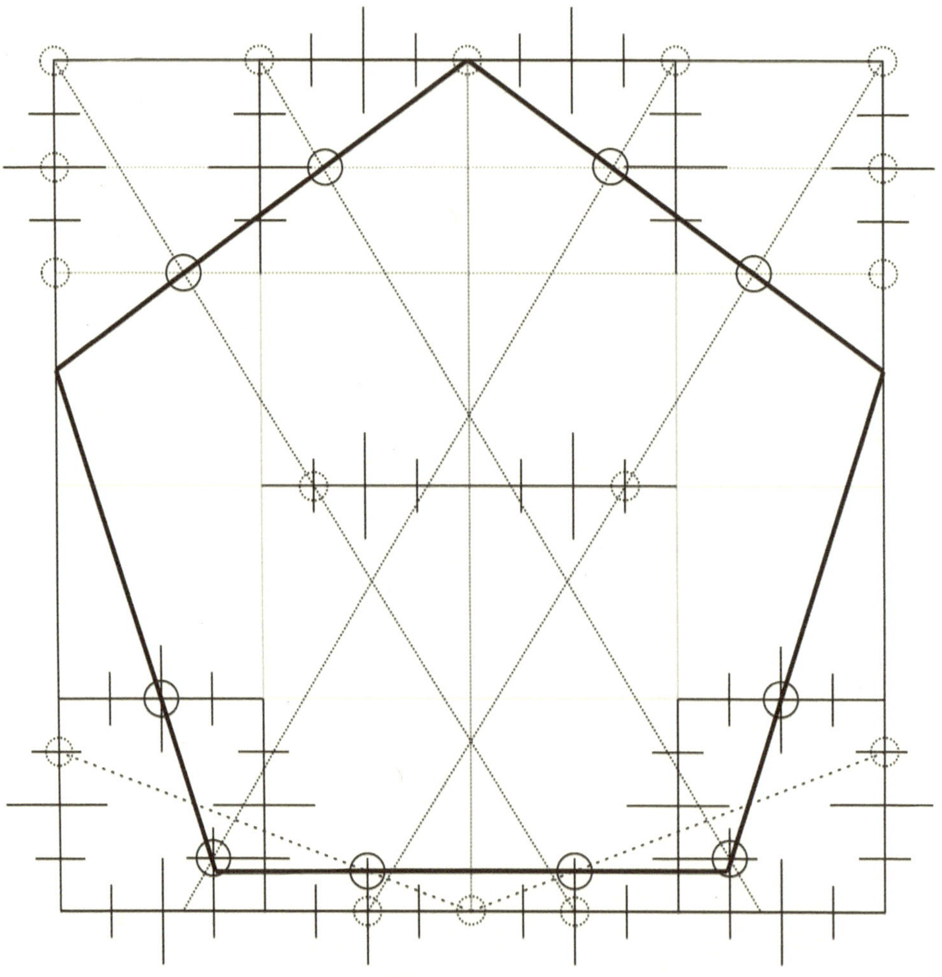

Folding paper in half is relatively easy to define and communicate. There is no guesswork in taking one end of a piece of paper to meet the opposite end of that same piece. Similarly, folding any two defined points to meet each other such that a crease would fall mid way between them is straightforward.

This design iterates that thinking through multiple levels, folding in half and in half again, always referencing previously defined points. Drawing lines would be equally effective to folding the lines that result from these iterations.

After defining a set of points by measuring half and half again across a grid, connecting the points defines the sides of a regular pentagon. These points are defined both independently, and in relation to other parts of the shape. In this way errors are not accumulated.

34 | Equilateral Triangle from Rectangle, Centered

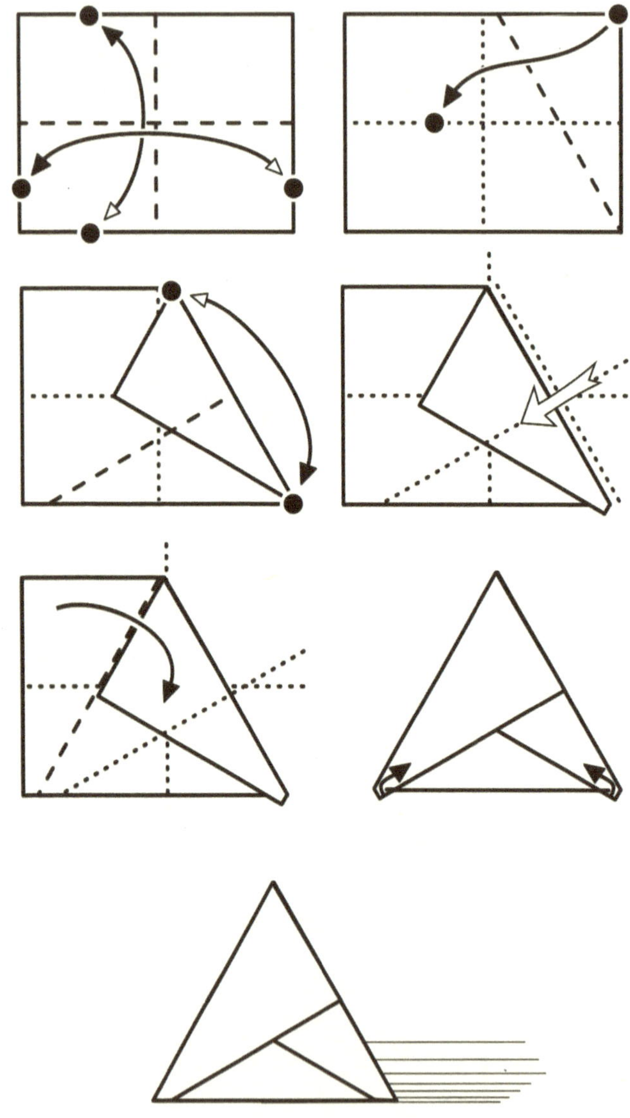

This design makes a triangle placed anywhere along the width of the paper. This diagram additionally illustrates centering the triangle.

In the first figure, the vertical line provides a reference for centering.

The second figure shows the traditional method of folding the top corner down to the center crease with the fold rooted at the bottom corner.

The middle row shows the new element, a fold perpendicular to the first side of the triangle. This fold defines a crease that acts like a guide track. The fold of the first side of the triangle can be moved back and forth by sliding the guide track crease along itself. In this instance the first side of the triangle is moved so the top intersects with the middle line.

The last set of figures shows the folding of the second side of the triangle, folding along the top edge of the first folded side. Then the extra bits extending below the triangle are folded up, resulting in the equilateral triangle.

35 | Equilateral Triangle, Truncated, from Square

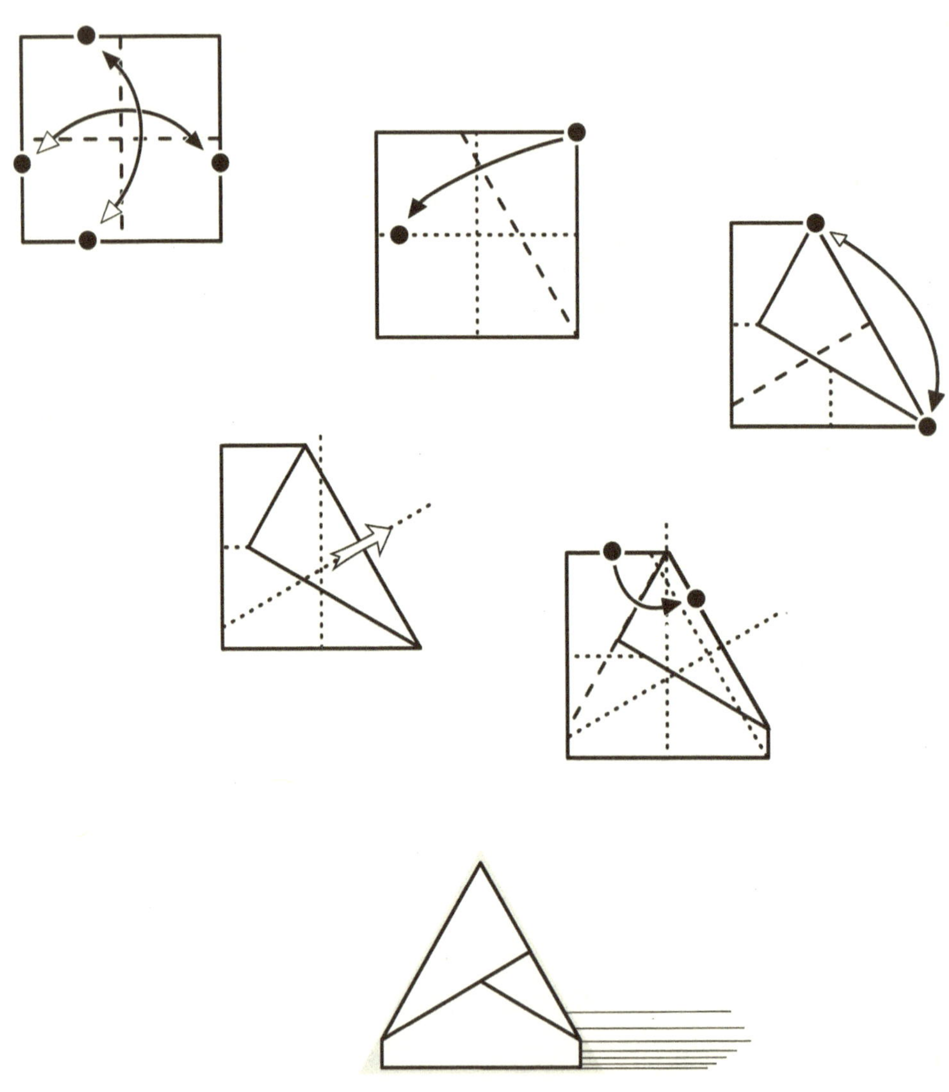

While a complete equilateral triangle is easy to arrive at, sometimes an almost complete equilateral triangle is sufficient. In this case the triangle formed is complete only excepting small parts of two corners.

This diagram makes use of the centering technique shown in the previous diagram. This allows one to find the 60 degree angle for the first side, then shift that side laterally so the other side can be folded to 60 degrees and both sides be the same size. This provides a large equilateral triangle missing only small parts of two points.

A challenge that I have taken on throughout this collection is maximizing the size of the final product relative to the starting paper size. Bigger designs from smaller paper.

While two points of this triangle are clipped, the fifth step may be skipped to create the same size triangle, with two complete points and only one truncated point. An example of this is shown in the design numbered 08, Tetrahedron Box with Lid.

38 | Maximal Hexagon from Square

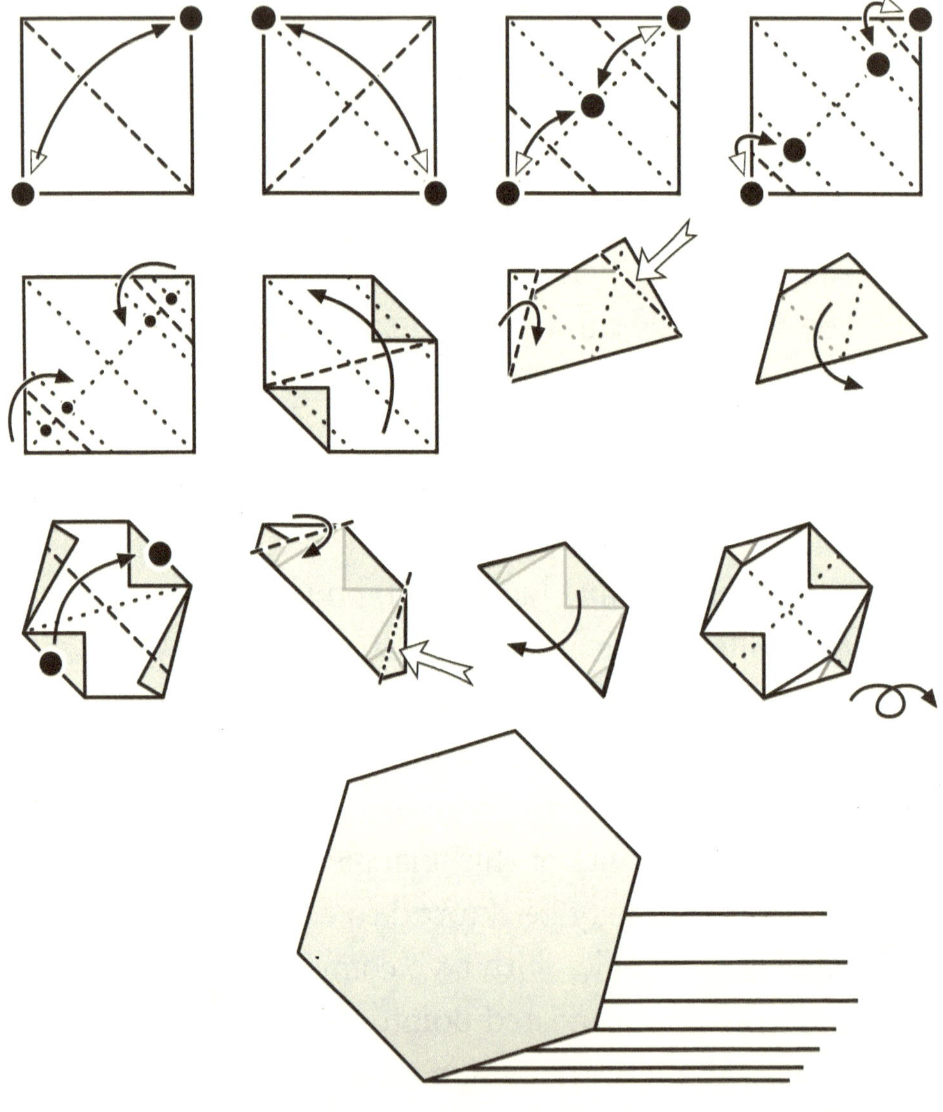

Mathematics defines this regular hexagon as the largest able to be inscribed in a square.

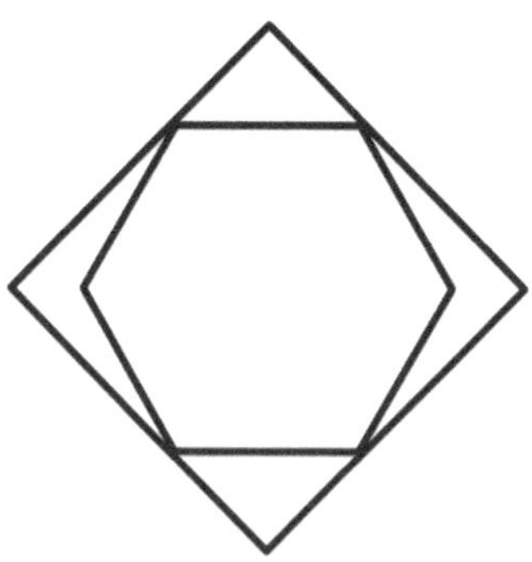

The first four steps of this diagram follow the simple and elegant pattern of halves between previously defined points.

The fifth figure uses large dots to indicate the creases marked are being folded to meet. This produces a fold midway between the first two creases.

These folds remain folded, with a next crease defined by the ends of those folds. Two side edges are then folded in, along the edges of the opposing half.

Next, the form is folded again and the overhanging tabs are folded along the edges of the opposing side.

Unfolding as shown results in a regular hexagon.

40 | Thirds, Halving One Corner

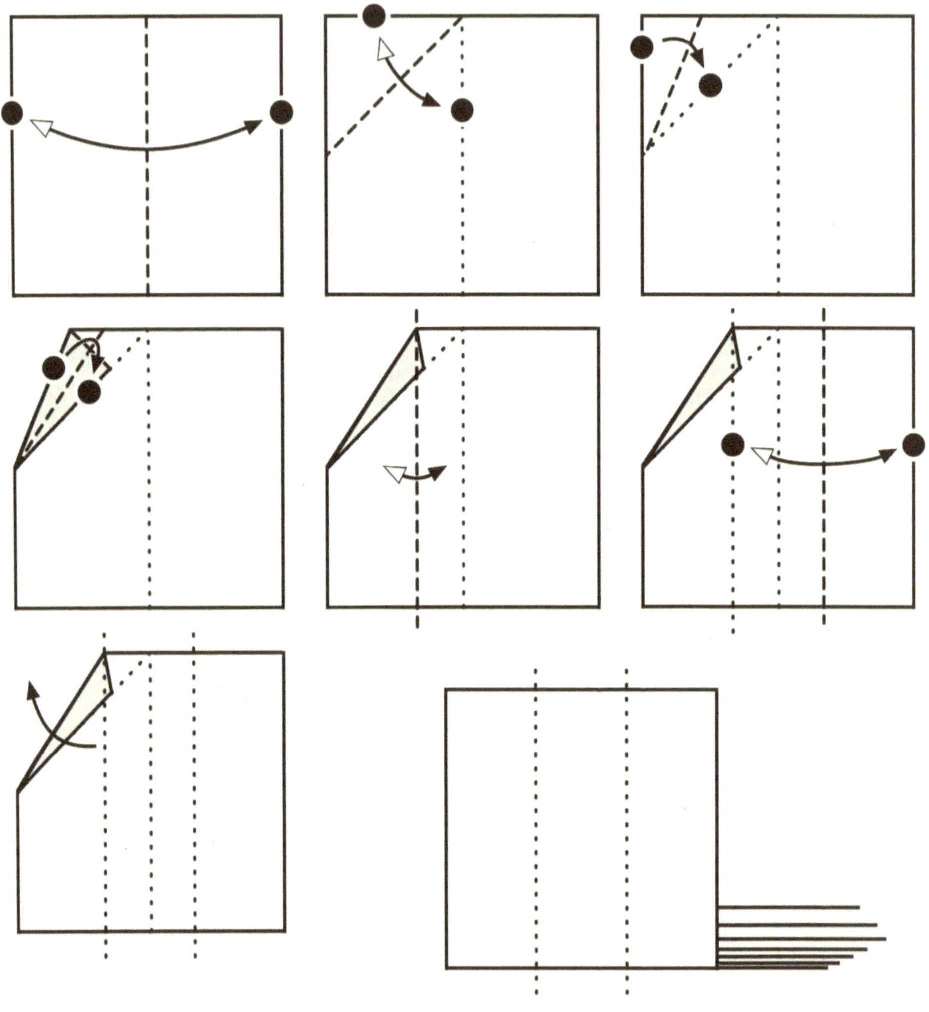

Here's a way to find the exact point one third across a paper sheet by folding one corner in half a few times.

As I design origami, my goal is to cut away all possible complexity. Defining points by halves and triangles accomplishes this.

Beginning in the first figure, the entire sheet is folded in half, one side over to meet the other and unfolded.

The top edge is then folded down to meet the center line crease, and then unfolded.
In the third figure the triangle just formed is folded in half, and then in the fourth figure, that folded section is folded in half. Where that fold intersects the top edge, that marks the point exactly one third across the top edge of the paper. The paper need not be perfectly square, nor need it be of any particular aspect ratio. Only the one side of the one corner is referenced to define the folds and finally define the one third point.

And now, some relevant math...

$$\frac{1}{3} = \frac{1}{4} + \frac{1}{16} + \frac{1}{64} + \frac{1}{256} + \cdots = \sum_{n=0}^{\infty} \frac{1}{4^{n+1}} = \frac{\frac{1}{4}}{1 - \frac{1}{4}}$$

Experimental

Sometimes a design comes together in a way that provides unexpected value.

Experiments are the beginning of designs. A question is asked, a fold is tried, a limitation found, and the question is refined.

Each design presented here is tangent to other designs in this collection. A path was developing toward an envelope or a tetrahedron and the path diverged. A few branches developed into a different tetrahedron, for example, or a different kind of envelope. One branch led to a design that was different. Those different designs are collected in this section.

Where a tetrahedron in progress makes a left turn to become a COVID-19 protective face mask, or an envelope is made into an unusual geometric form—this is where folds inside the box are made from outside of the box.

06 | Rolling Oloid

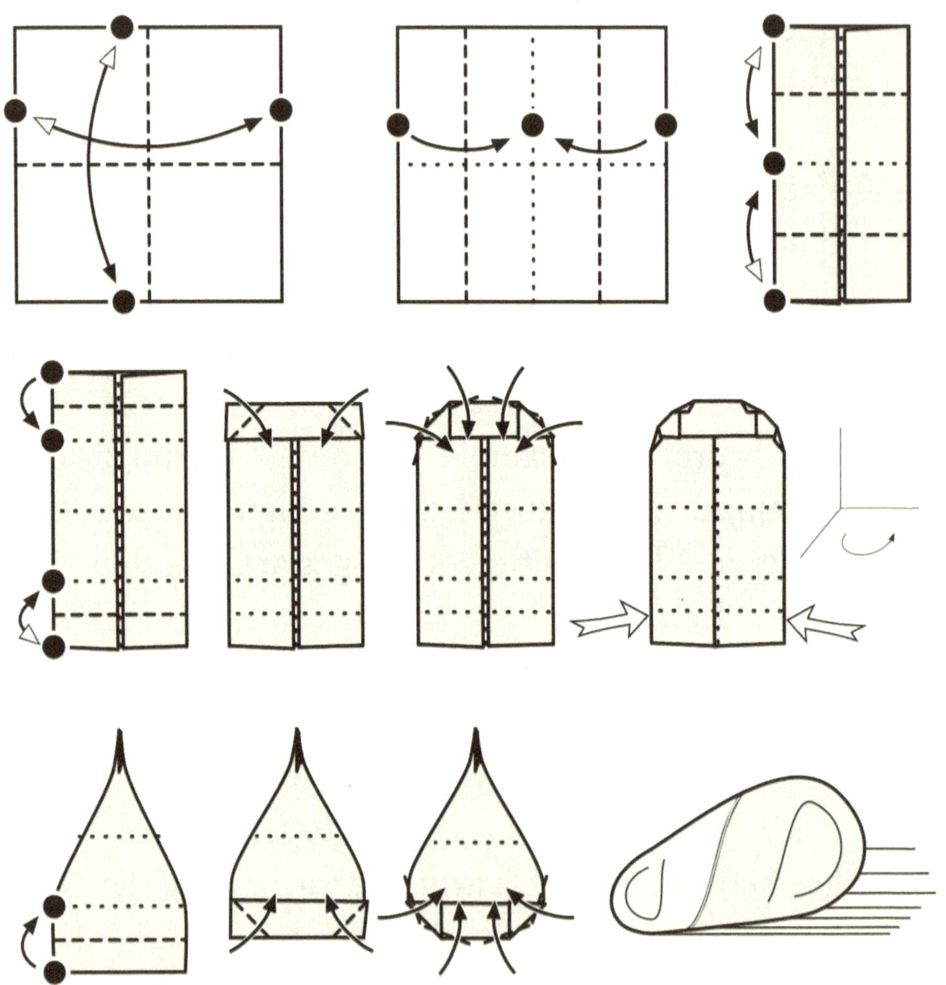

For anyone who has stressed over whether to spend the extra money for a cast and polished solid brass oloid or wait a while for a plastic oloid to 3D print, here is the optimal solution.

An investment perfectly aligned with the term of sustained engagement one would likely experience, the cost of this oloid is one sheet of paper and about five minutes.

Rolling an oloid down an incline really is fun, both wobbly and smooth, chaotic and rock solid at the same time.

With origami, all that's needed is a sheet of paper. No need for expensive manufacturing, materials and shipping charges.

Of course, if you've never heard of an oloid...

Anyway...

09 | Face Mask

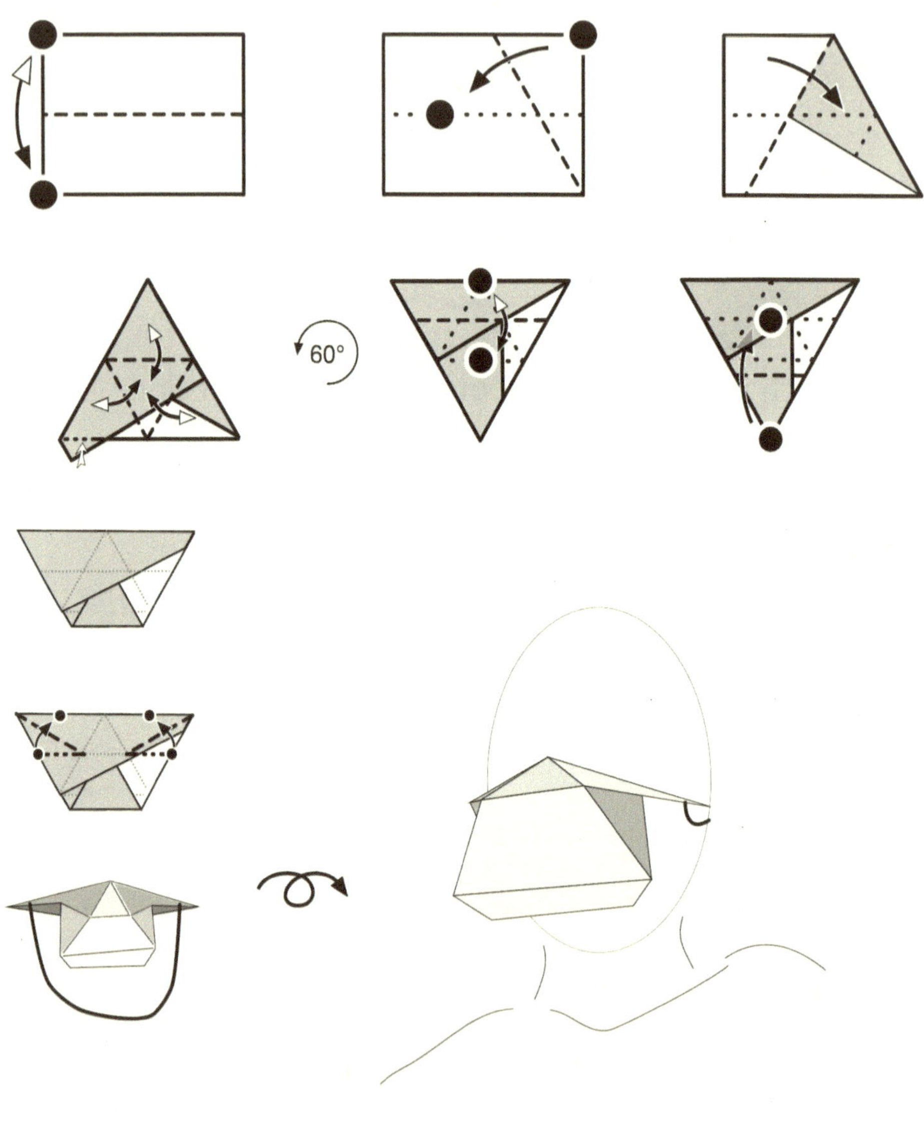

This is about the biggest complete tetrahedron possible from a single sheet of paper.

Several diagrams illustrate the folding of an equilateral triangle, further folded into equilateral triangles.

The triangle is carefully collapsed into itself, leaving a panel on top with two half triangle tabs.

A final step lowers the panel onto the tetrahedron, and inserts the two half triangle tabs inside the tetrahedron. Those tabs are then folded back onto the inside of the wall of the tetrahedron, locking the form together.

One edge of this design remains unsealed.

Two of these tetrahedrons may be nested in an offset arrangement to form a fully sealed container.

12 | Dollar Vulture

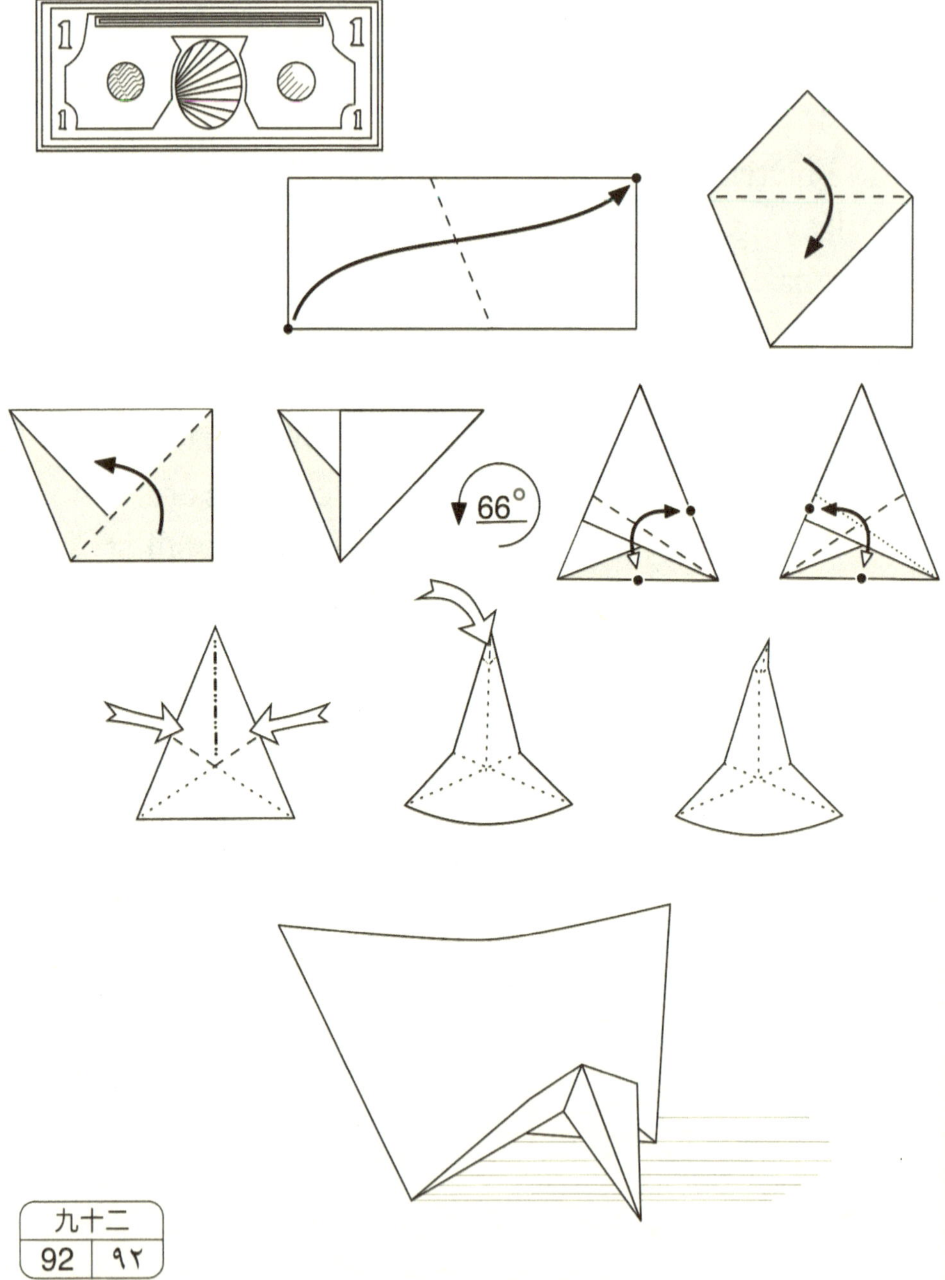

Dollar Vulture takes inspiration from triangles, of course, and also my series of children's books featuring Fluffy the Vulture.

One evening the challenge presented to fold a stack of dollar bills into origami to add visual interest as they were being presented as gifts.

Time being limited, the further challenge was to design a form that became recognizable with a minimum of folds.

First, the dollar bill is folded in half on an angle with two opposite corners being brought together. The remaining two corners are folded in, as shown, to form a triangle. Now the triangle is rotated so the short side is on the bottom. Fold that bottom edge up to meet each of the long sides, unfolding each time. In the last row, three figures show how the form is pinched into a bird shape. The top end, the beak or head of the vulture, is defined by simply bending it down.

Fold the triangle, throw in two more folds, then pinch, bend and it's done.

24 | Star from Any Polygon, Edge Locked Pleats

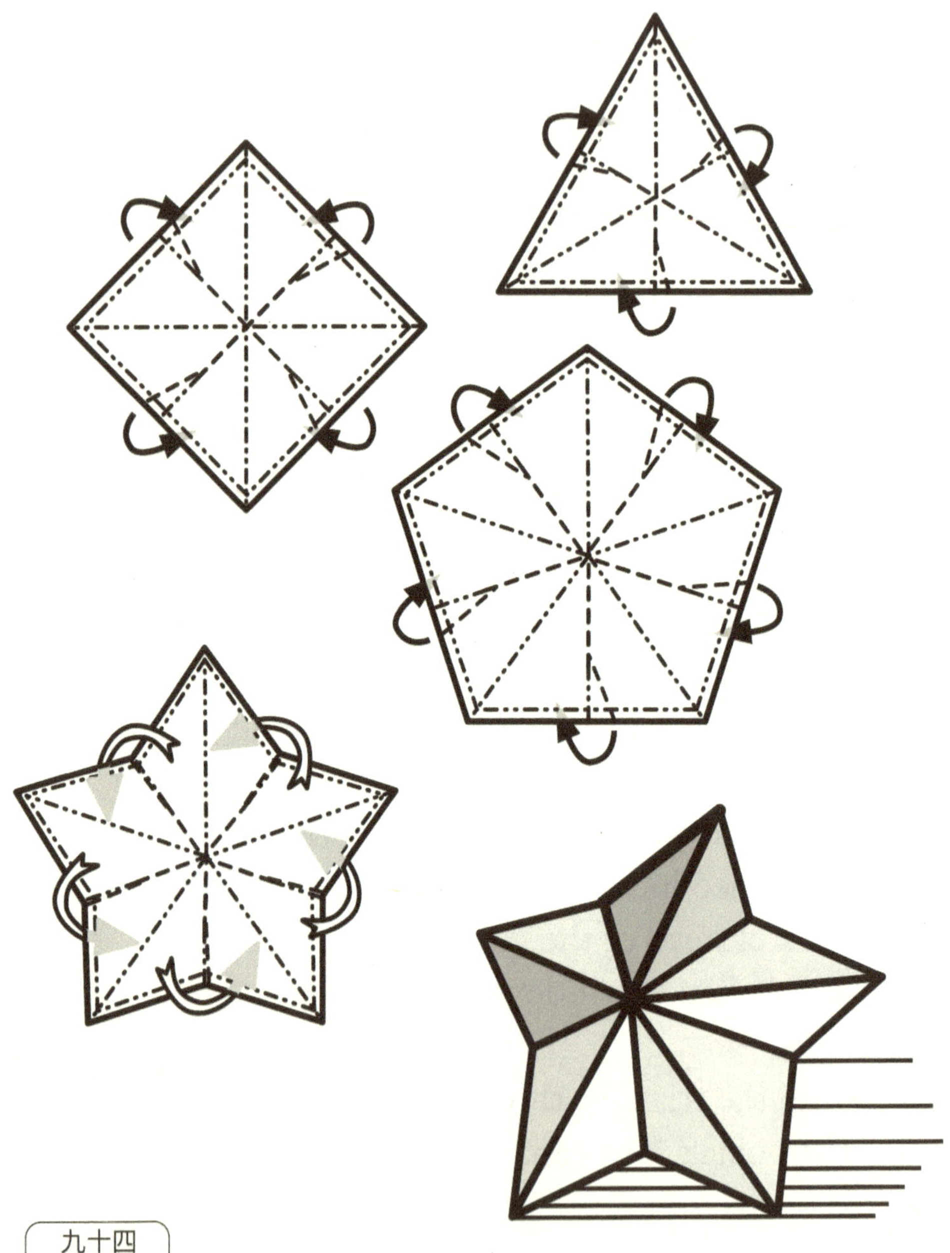

Here's a quick design for a three dimensional star.

The length of the points are proportional to the thickness of the center.

Start with any polygon. The sides determine the number and length of the points of the star.

Folds terminating at the hub and at a corner of the polygon are mountain folds. These form the points of the star.

Between the points, a valley fold originates at the hub and terminates a short distance before the side edge of the polygon. That same line then continues to the edge as a mountain fold, with a slightly divergent branch continuing nearly parallel as a valley fold. The divergent valley fold gathers material, adding definition to the points of the star.

Folding down the outside edge locks in place the folds from center to edge that define the points of the star. This outside edge fold can also be used to join two like stars back to back.

25 | Star from Any Polygon, Squashed Pleats

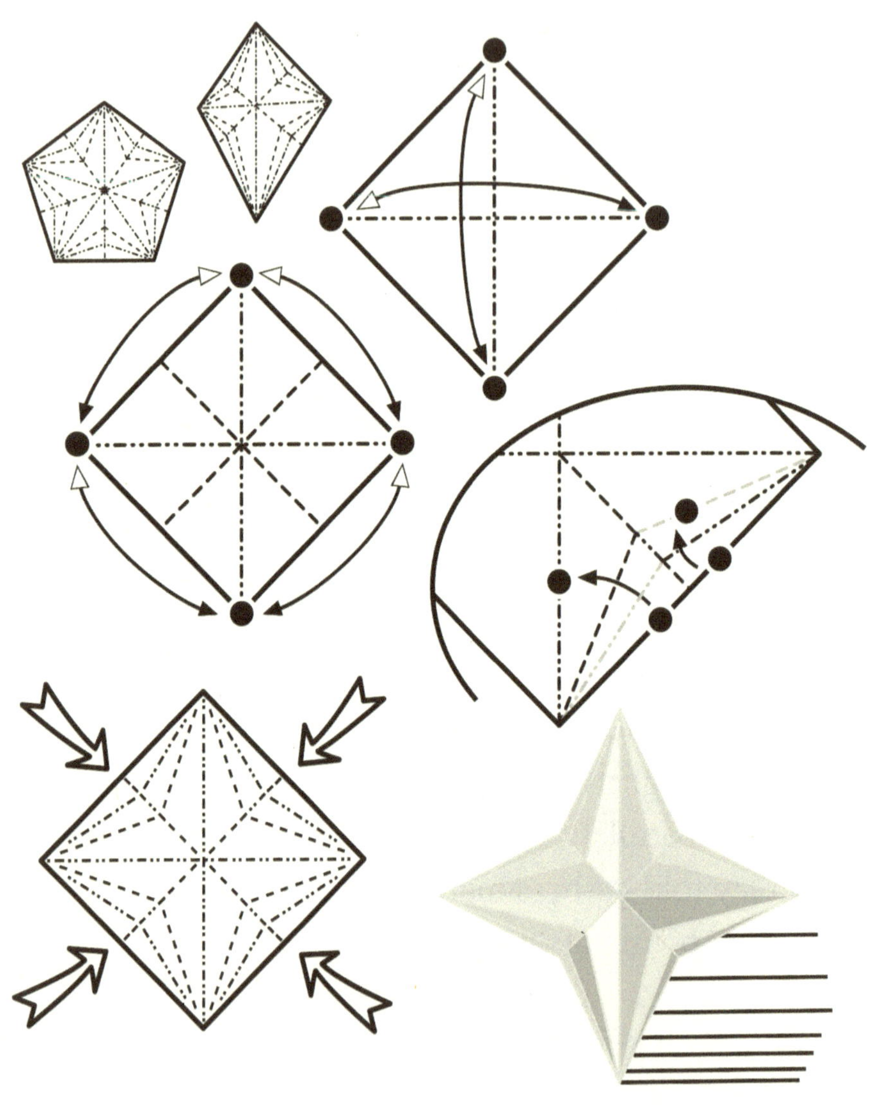

Twinkling points make this design shine brightly, as much as folded paper can.

A faceted surface is formed by intersecting folds that both form the star and lock the form in place. Any polygon can form the base of this star.

In this diagram, the star illustrated is based on a square. Creases run from the hub or center of the star to the sides on the outer edge.

The inset, middle row, right side, presents a magnified view of the folds that may be made between the points. Note the crease from the center to the edge changes from valley fold to mountain fold and back as it crosses the pleats.

A series of folding triangles in half is used to define the form. Pushed together as illustrated, the pleats fold in toward the center of the star, defining the points of the star while minimizing overall thickness or depth of the form.

47 | Reciprocating Constant Airflow Fan

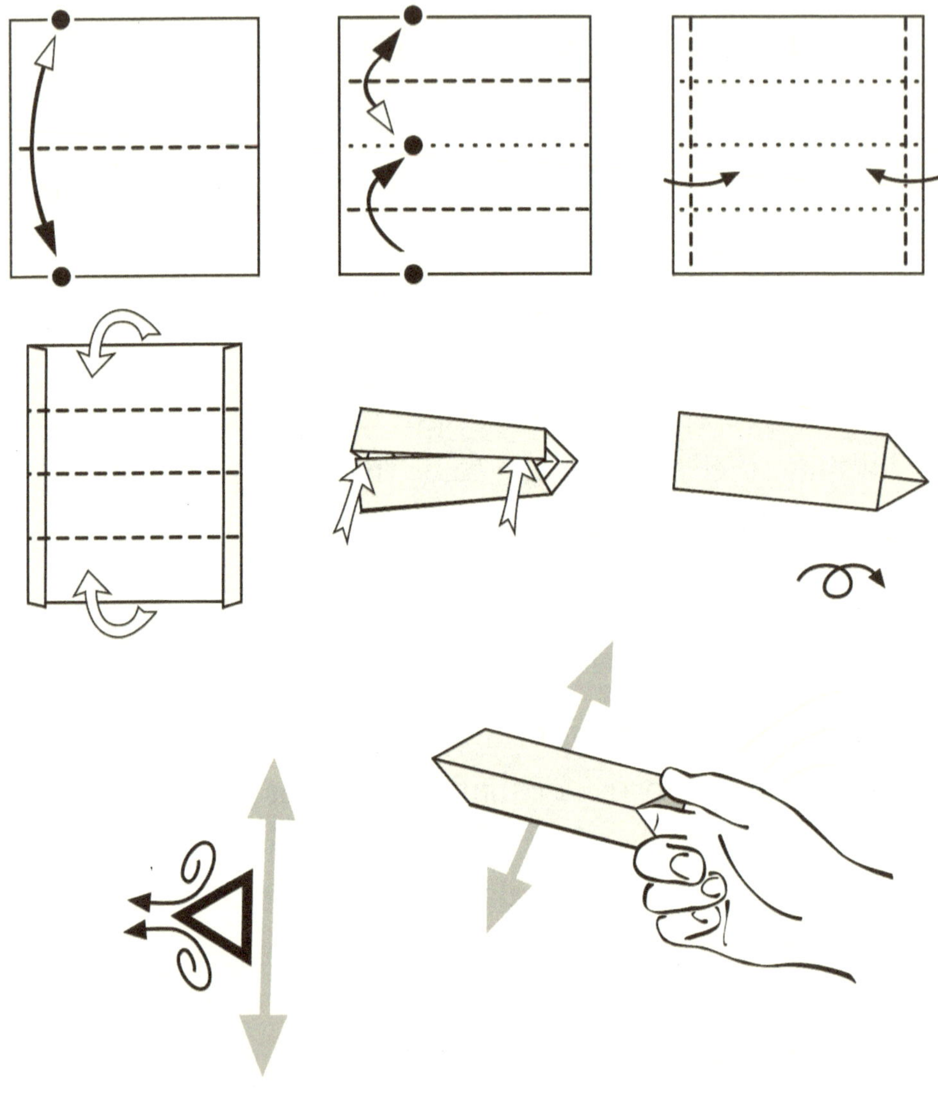

Here is a diagram of a three sided extruded triangle form.

The diagram shows how four panels are formed, along with a folded over edge. When folded into itself, the first and last panels slide together into the channel formed by the folded over ends.

When this shape moves up and down as pictured in the diagram, it pushes whatever fluid it is moving through. When it moves up, it pushes fluid left. When it moves down, it pushes fluid left also. More commonly, like with a fan blade, the direction the fluid is pushed would reverse when the direction of the fan blade was reversed.

Up would push fluid left, down would push fluid right, for example.

Now the question arises—what would be a practical use for an unusual fan blade like this?

Perhaps a very large pendulum arm with this shape, and as it swings from side to side a gentle constant breeze is felt by those nearby.

Envelopes

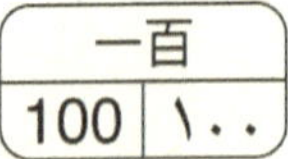

Playing around with the foundational triangle, an envelope form became evident. Corners folded in and interlocked resulted in an envelope that is as secure as it is complicated and overdone. In more recent designs my focus is minimalist design with maximal size.

The initial design, Rectangle Envelope, was published by OrigamiUSA in their Origami Collection 2022. Having this original design published, that I was able to diagram, was a great encouragement.

Included in this section are cylinder based designs, which at first glance may not make sense. In fact, the cuffed top edge locking in the form of some of these envelopes led directly to the Cylinder and Funnel designs.

07 | Rectangle Envelope

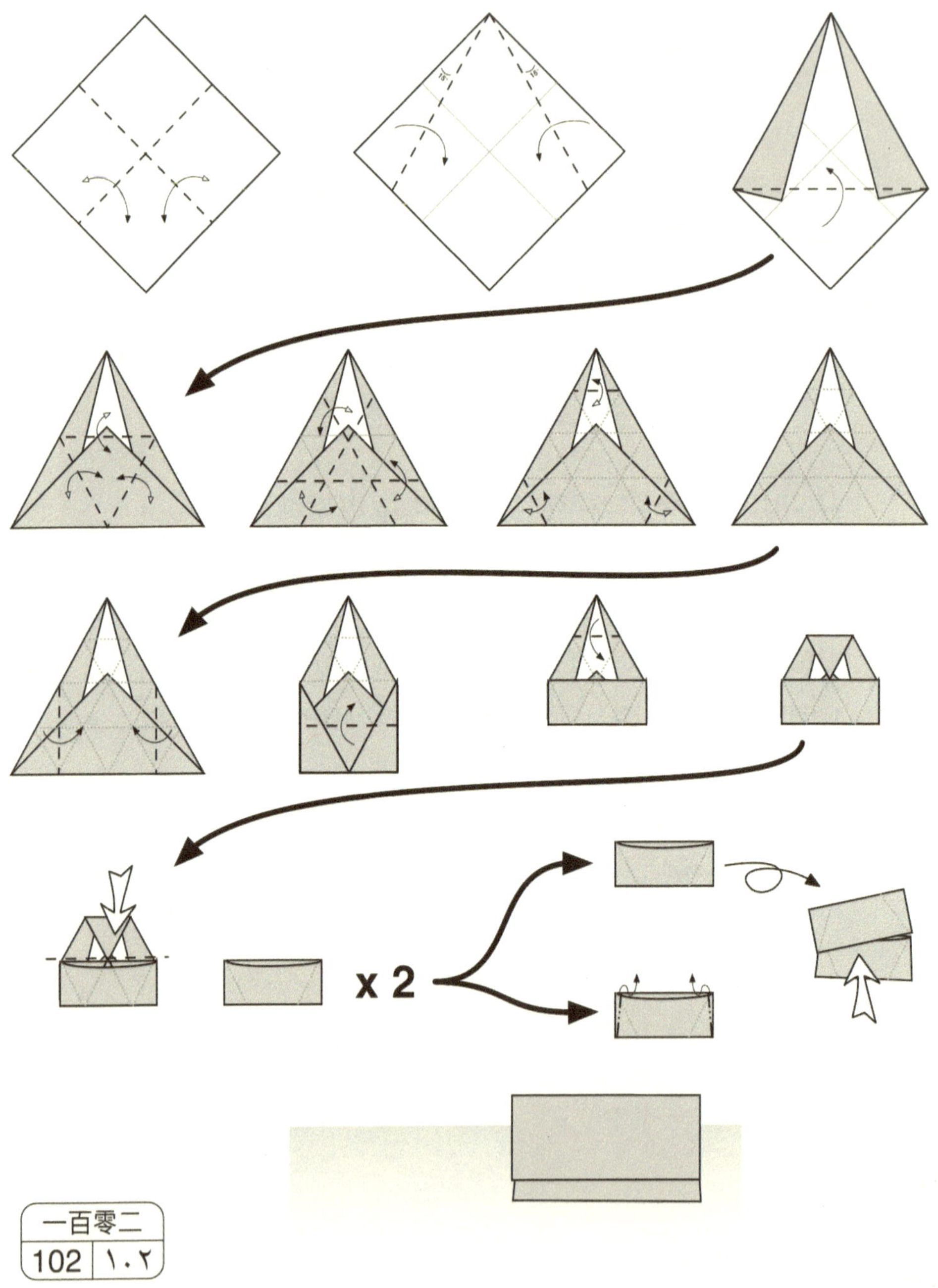

Published:
OrigamiUSA
Origami Collection 2022
Page 218

It was certainly encouraging to have this original design and diagram published.

This design illustrates how, sometimes, inefficiency in a part of the system makes the system more effective.

For the size of the resulting envelope, there is an awful lot of paper required. The final envelope has multiple layers due to the number of overlapping folds.

Starting with a triangle provides an unusual design, in line with the overall theme of this collection.

27 | Inside Out Envelope

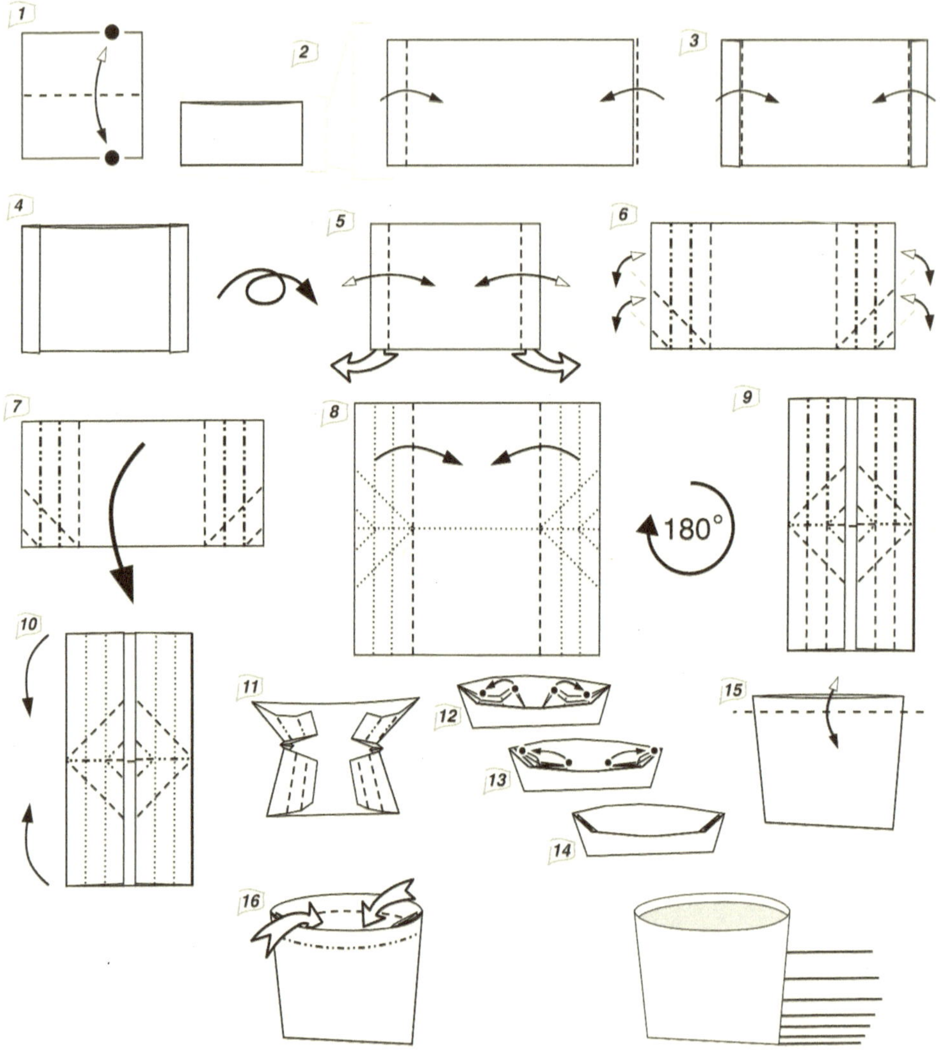

1 2 3 4 5 6 7 8 9 180° 10 11 12 13 14 15 16

Published:
The Fold
the online magazine of OrigamiUSA
Issue 82, May–June 2024

Folds, and in particular interlocking folds, are required to create a three dimensional object from a substantially two dimensional piece of paper.

The object of this design was to turn an otherwise simple design for a bag or envelope inside out. All of the functional folds are put inside the envelope, keeping the faces of the envelope clean.

There are many variations possible on the theme presented in this diagram.

29 | Cylinder

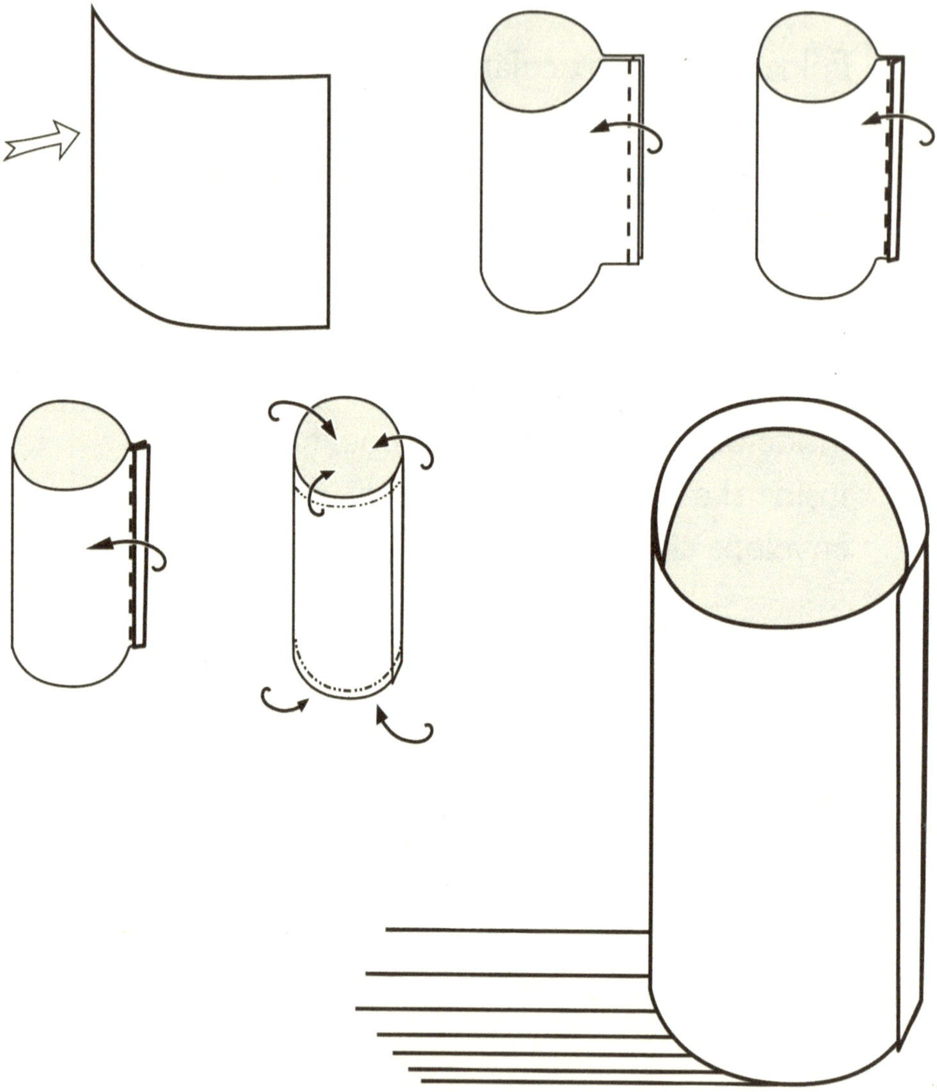

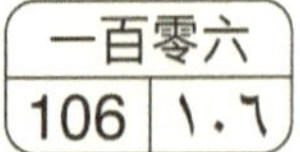

Folding a cylinder seems counterintuitive, even moreso to say that triangles were involved at any point.

This design is inspired by the envelope designs that are part of this collection. While the envelopes do in fact include triangles, none are directly applied in the cylinder.

Imagine a thin sheet of paper, with opaque designs applied by drawing or other means. That sheet then folded into a cylinder could sit on top of and around a tiny battery powered light and provide an illuminated decorative shade.

An interesting side benefit of the cylinder design is the ability to create an extrusion-like form, adding folds along the length. This is like a cookie cutter, and could be of any height. Shorter lengths tend to be more stable, as the intersection of the cuff fold and the side seam fold provides stability.

30 | Funnel

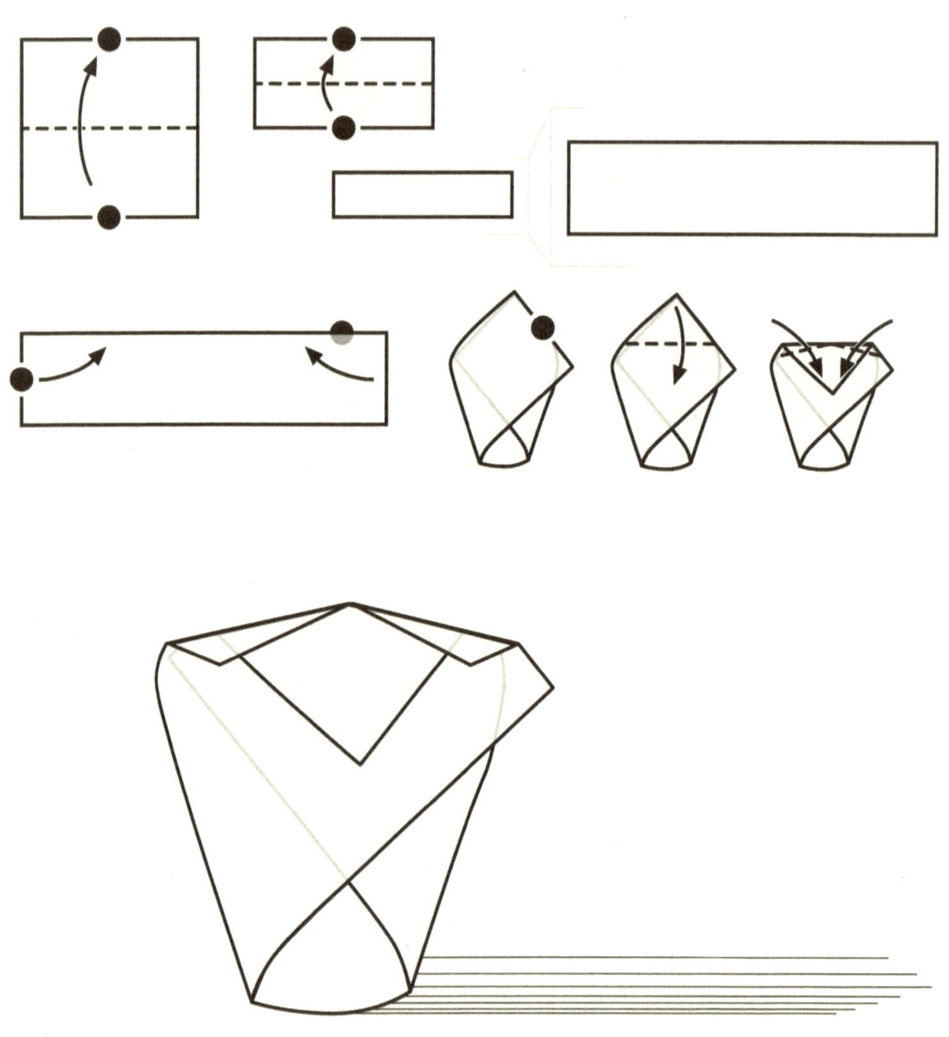

Funnels are extremely useful in the kitchen, and can save a lot of time and effort.

This design provides an extremely quick way to fold a piece of paper into a funnel that won't come apart, and can be set into a jar or bottle without having to hold it in place. There are two stages in this design.

First, the elongated rectangle must be obtained. There are many ways to accomplish this, with folding from a square illustrated.

In the second stage, the ends of the strip are brought together as illustrated. One short end is bent back and twisted slightly to aligned with the other end of the long side.

After the cone segment is formed, the top edge is folded over with non-parallel folds locking each other in place.

32 | Cone Inside Out Envelope

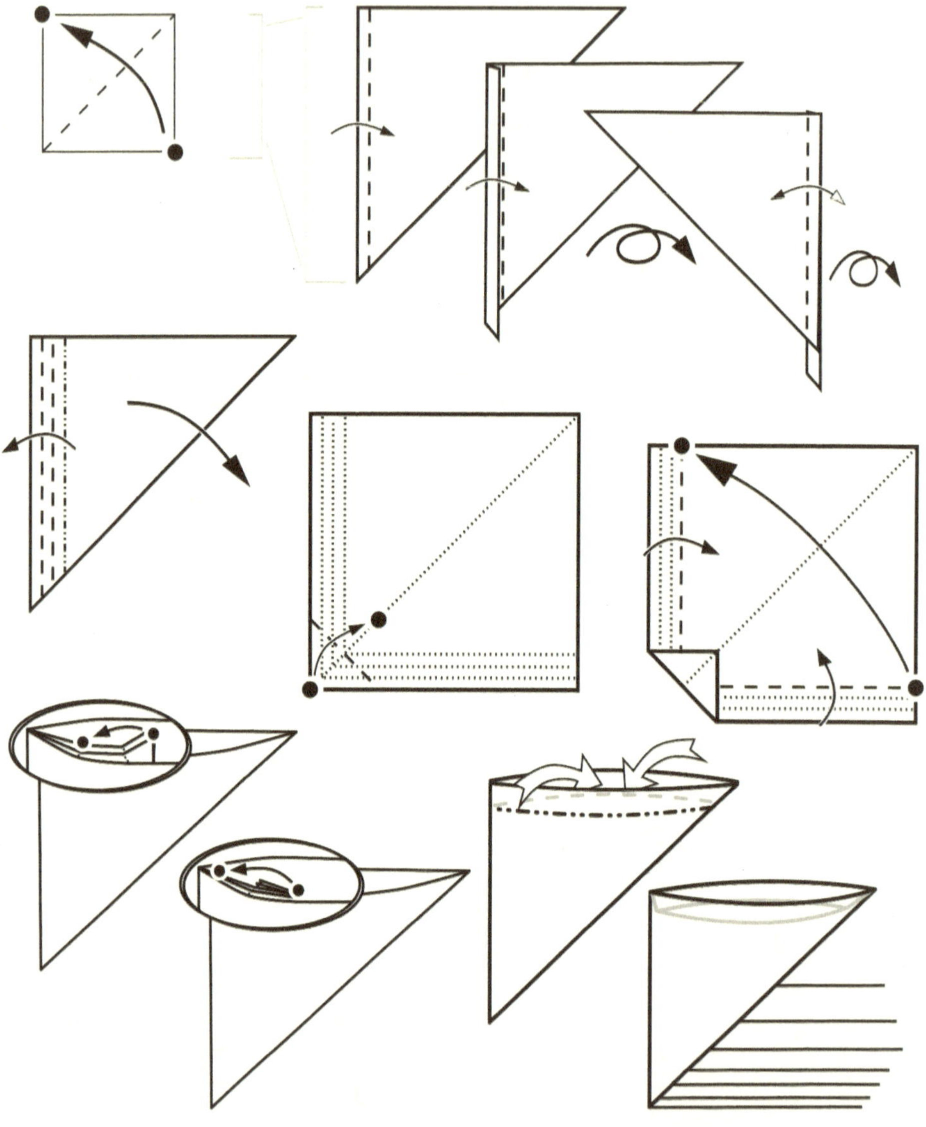

Here is diagrammed a square, folded in half along a diagonal, then sealed by rolling a seam along one side and cuffed along the other side to secure the form.

Paper cone packaging is used with freshly prepared snack foods, as a holder for ice cream cones, or even as a single use drinking water cup.

This cone design has a single secure seam that requires no tape or glue.

With only one seam, it is faster to make than rectangular envelope packages with two seams.

For lightweight applications such as popcorn one might even simplify the seam, folding it just once instead of over again.

33 | Self Sealed Envelope

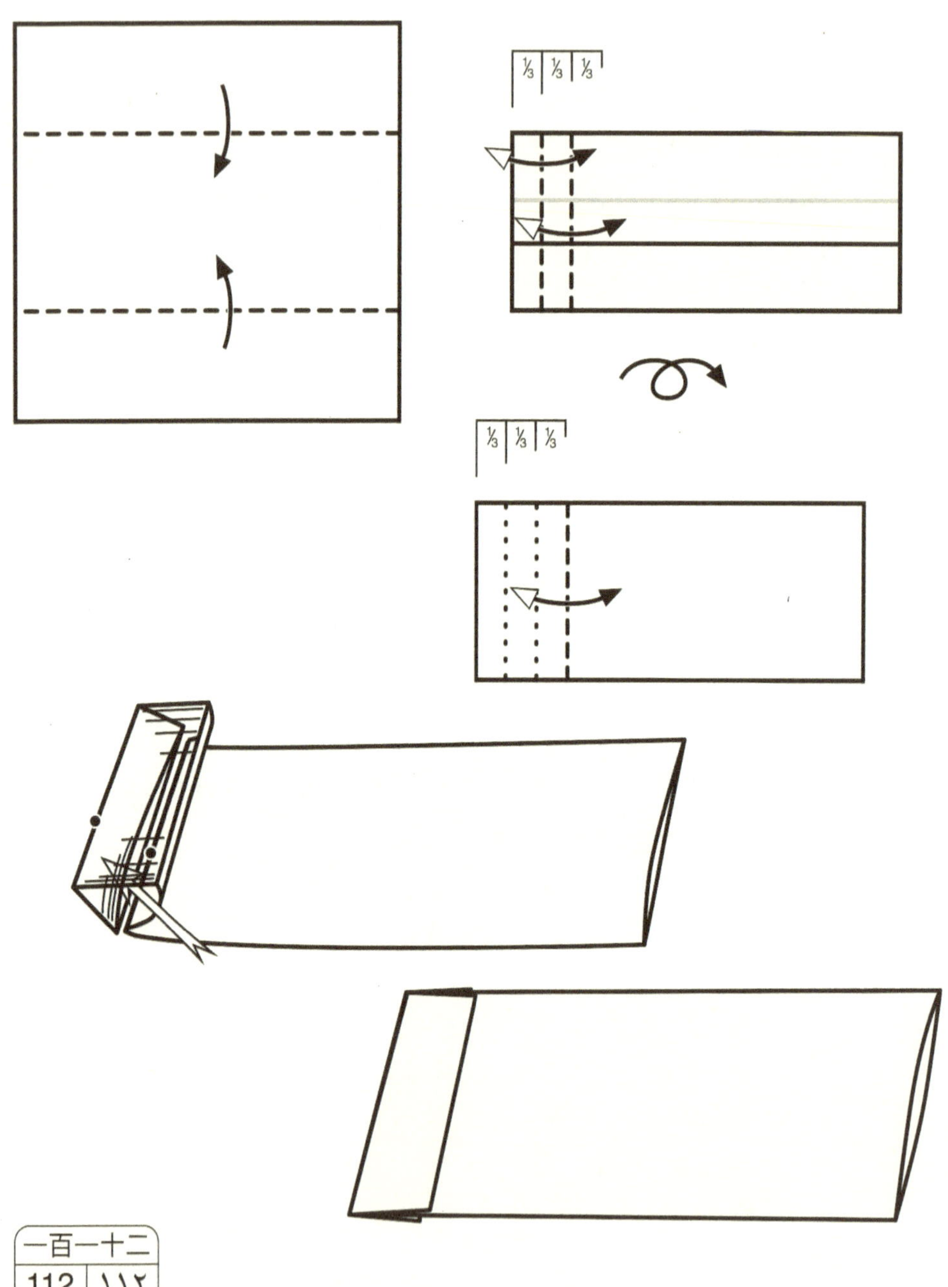

In a way, the thinking behind this design started with the ouroboros, an image of a snake-like animal forming a circle, eating its own tail, illustrating a cyclic view of life.

Likewise I imagined the open end of an envelope closing over itself. Cuffs were already being used to finish the open ends, and so my design process started looking at ways to modify the cuff in three dimensions. If the cuff could somehow cover the seam with itself that might be the most elegant answer. This, of course, did not fully make sense. Further pursuing the idea of using the open seam to cover itself, I looked for a way to bring the open end back around so as to slide over that same end of the envelope. Folding, and using more material than I had hoped would be needed, was the answer that is diagrammed here.

Transparency is used in the fourth figure to show what is happening in between layers of paper. While not entirely realistic, this is designed to help the reader visualize an otherwise hidden placement of one fold back into the open end.

44 | Triangle Closure for Envelopes

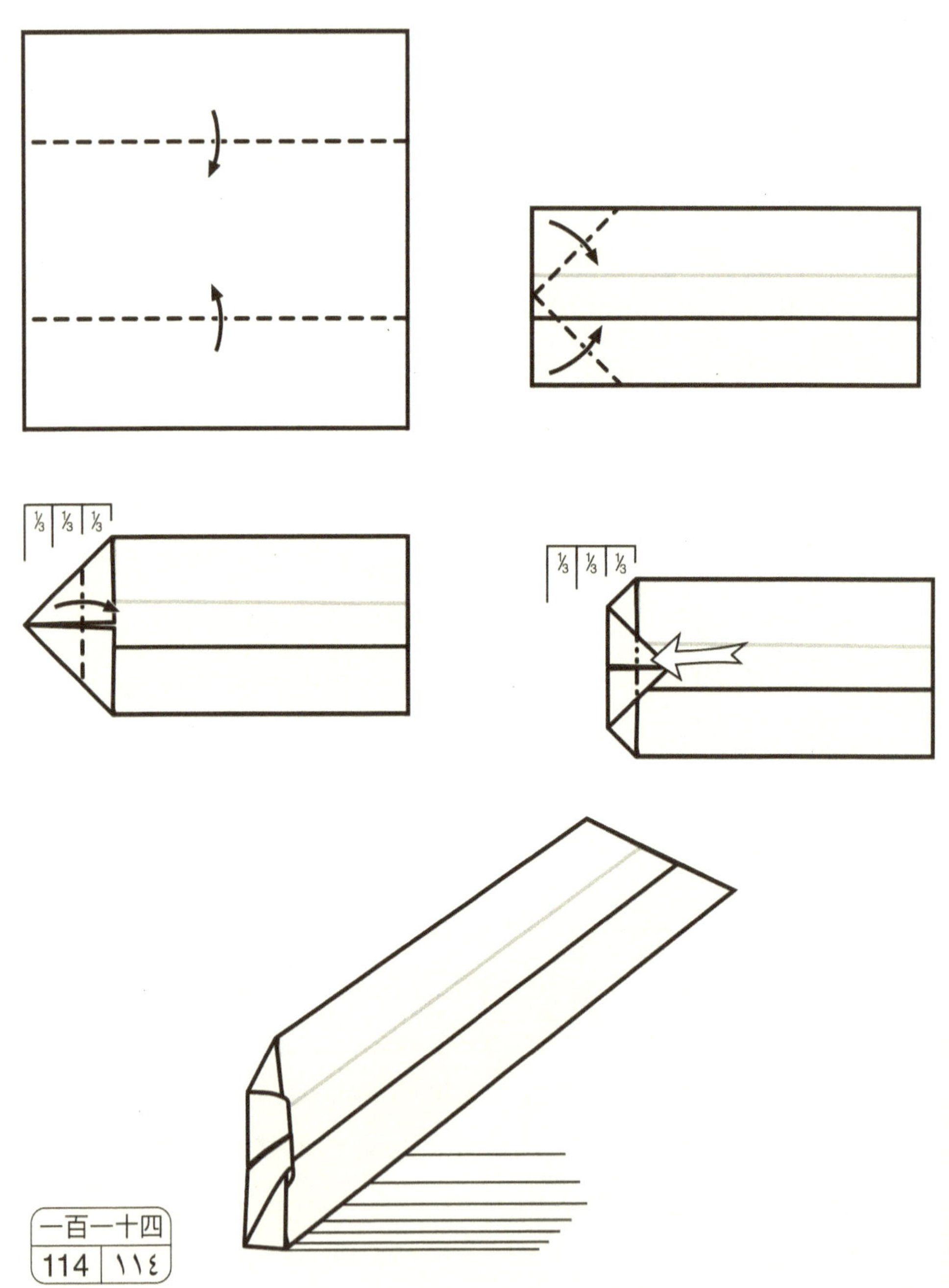

Here is a novel approach to securing the open end of an envelope with only minimal folds. To my knowledge, and after a diligent search, this design has not previously been published. While a clip or tape is common enough and certainly functional, this provides a means of securely closing an envelope, packet or paper bag simply and with nothing extra.
The construction of the envelope or bag is not important. Any form that terminates in a generally flat cylinder with generally straight edges should work with this closure design.

Folding this closure begins with, and this should be no surprise, triangles. Folding the corners down and into the center is illustrated in the first few figures. The center point then formed is folded down twice, with the creases at 1/3 intervals. The first folds two thirds of the point back toward the body of the envelope. The second folds one third, the end of the point, back under itself to lock the folded end in place.

36 | Stand Up Envelope

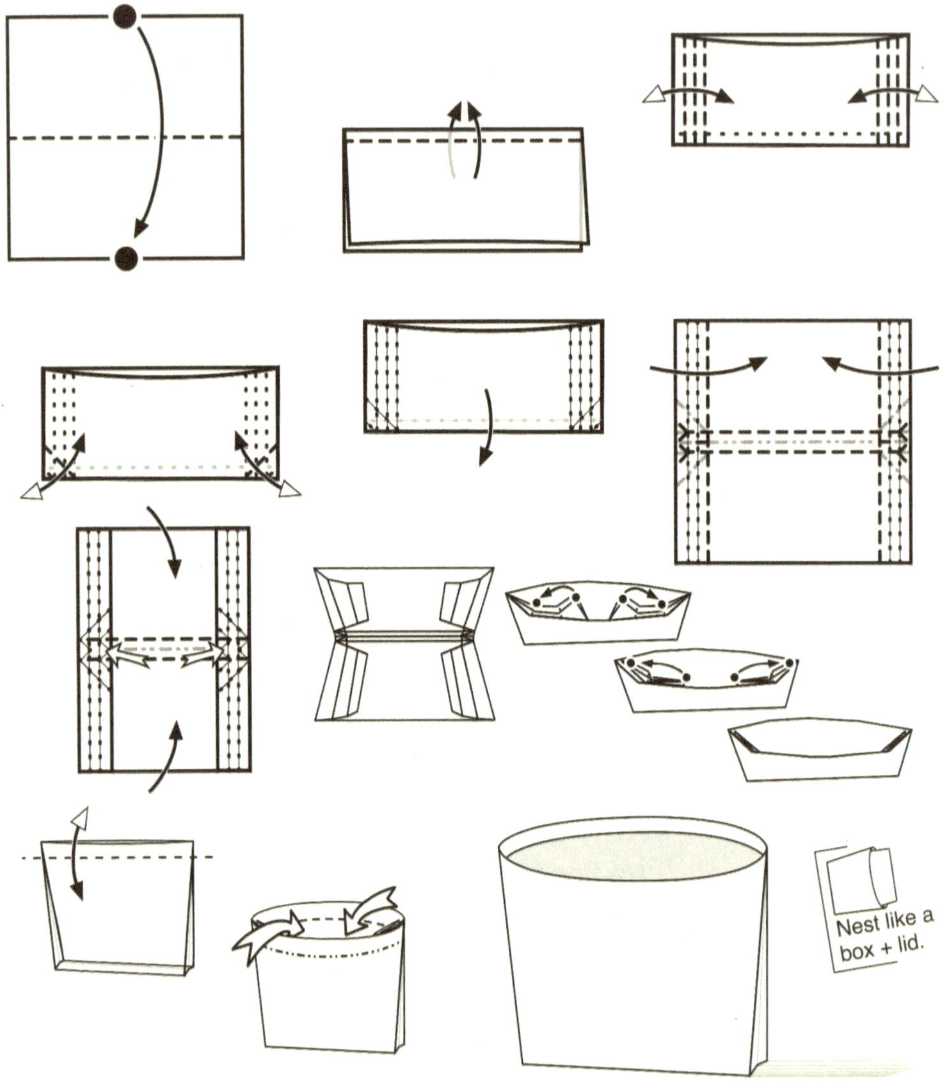

Nest like a box + lid.

While seemingly a trivial modification, the addition of a gusset at the bottom of this envelope design significantly changes the finished dimensions of the envelope and allows one to make a stand up bag or even a nested envelope box.

The crease pattern seems complicated, even though the steps to create the pattern are relatively simple.

The first and second figure illustrate the folding of the bottom pleat. This defines the depth of the final envelope, front to back. The sides need no such additional pleat.

The following steps illustrate the side folds. Figure six illustrates the crease pattern that is arrived at through the first five steps. It is at this point, having unfolded the paper, the sides are now folded in while in figure seven simultaneously refolding the bottom pleat.

Regroup and pay careful attention to the crease pattern, mountain and valley folds, if anything doesn't seem right.

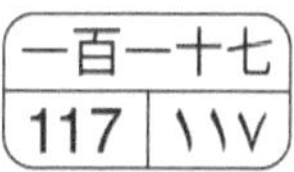

49 | Locking Strap

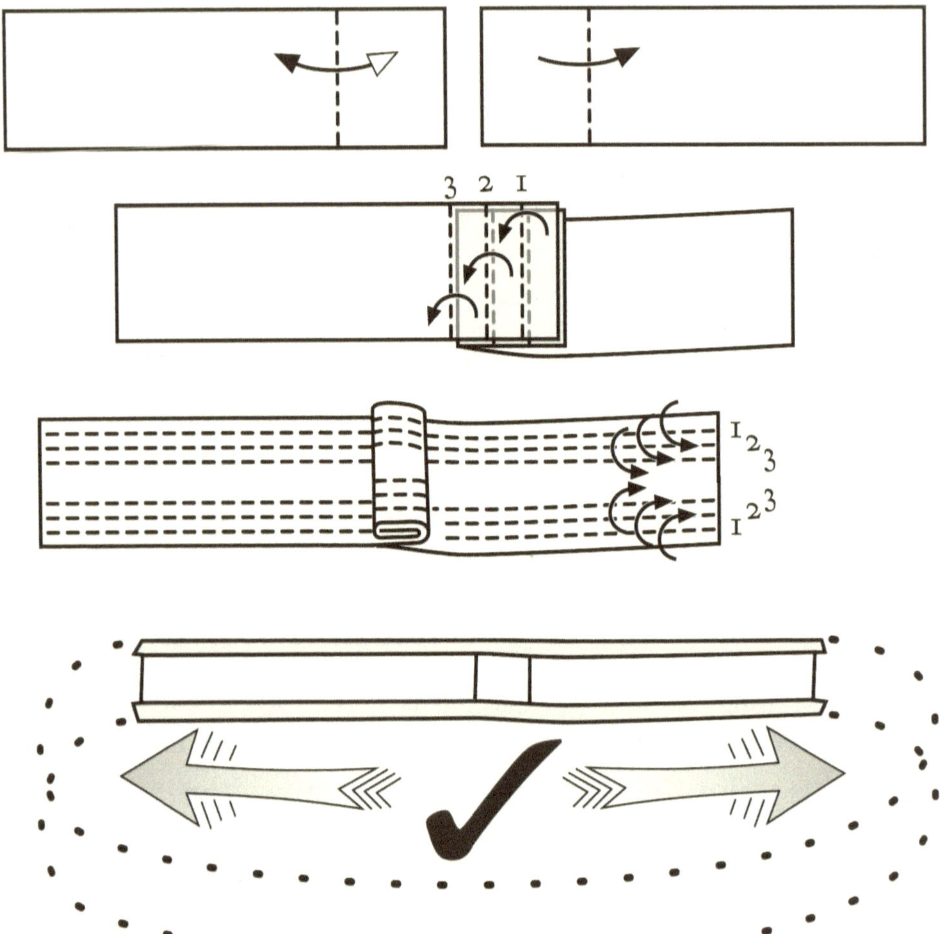

Origami inspires engineering solutions in spacecraft, robotics and even household items. Engineering challenges are met with origami designs that provide seam integrity, structural strength, the ability to transform from densely compact to open and functional.

Here is presented a folded seam that joins two panels such that failure is only possible if the material itself is compromised.

Folding begins with long rectangles. Two ends are overlapped and rolled together with a series of three folds. This could be two ends of the same long rectangle, or two discrete long rectangles. Locking in these folds is a set of perpendicular folds along the length of the paper. Once all of these folds are set, they cannot be pulled apart without the paper itself tearing.

Under the right conditions, this seam can even be formed in place and under tension, securing a strap around something.

50 | Fast Package

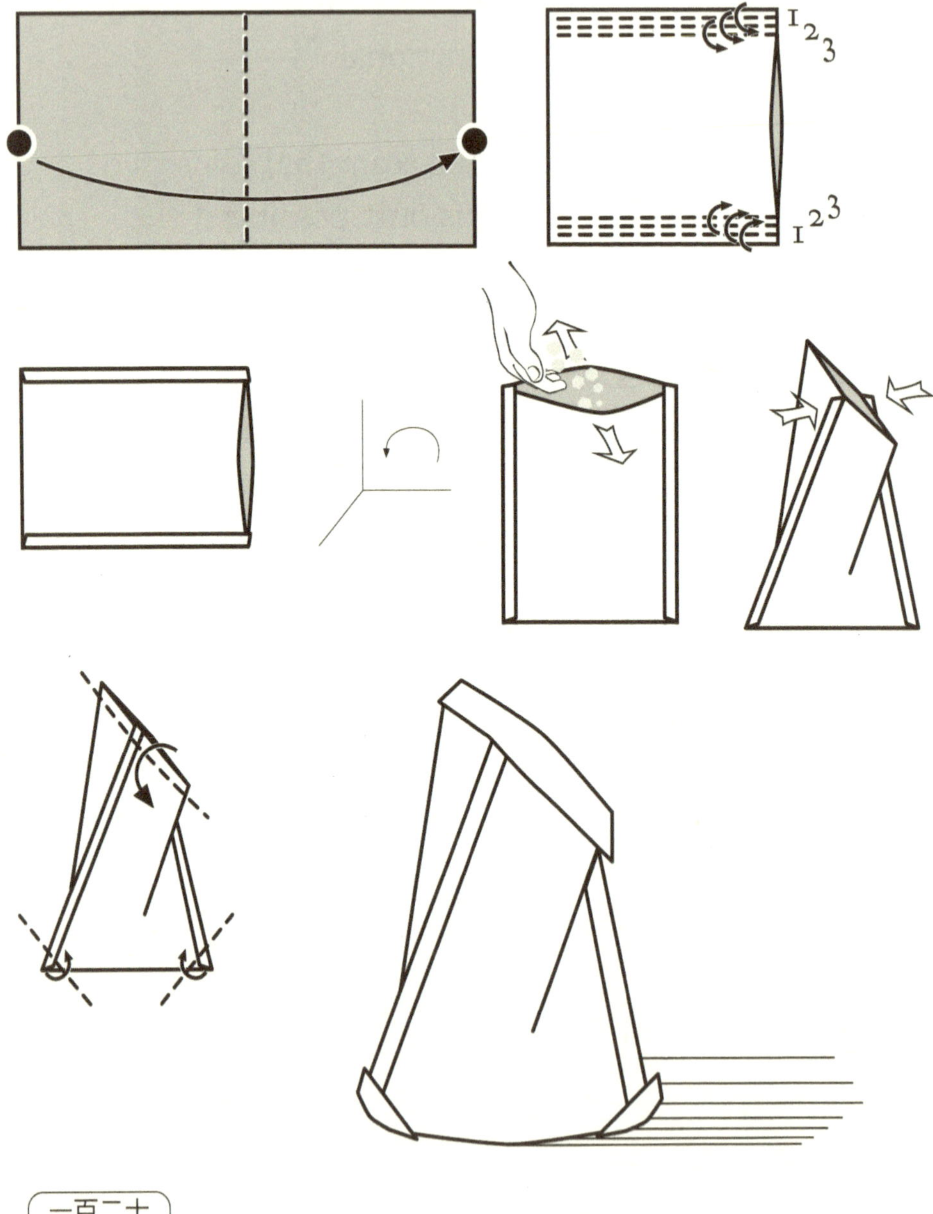

Quick and dirty solutions are often the most useful, not because they are better but because they are ready.

At a restaurant, a paper placemat may be folded into a take out bag. Preparing for a party, one could quickly fold sheets of colorful paper into gift bags.

In this design rough measurements combine with a carefully designed structure.
Based on the Inside Out Envelope, this design leaves all of the folds on the outside of the package so fewer steps are required.
Filling the envelope, illustrated in the central figure, is followed by flattening the open end to form a tetrahedron. This brings together the side seams at the middle of the open end such that they can be folded together. The perpendicular arrangement of the top fold and side seam folds locks the fold in place.
Folding in the corners of the bottom of the package provides added stability.

Paper Airplanes

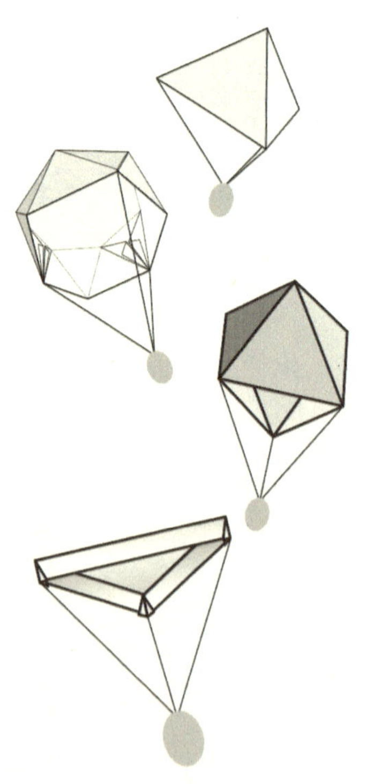

Origami entered my consciousness when, as a very young child, I played with paper airplanes.

The dining room table was the drafting table, factory floor and hangar where aircraft were designed, built and maintained.

At that table my grandmother taught me the basics of paper airplane design. My original diagram of the traditional plane she taught me is presented in this collection.

This reminds me of another toy she taught me to make—a weighted parachute. Originally this exercise in basic aerodynamics consisted of a silk handkerchief tied to a heavy wooden clothespin. I wonder how that contributed to my interest in paper airplanes. On the facing page I've imagined a few origami parachute toys using designs from this collection.

Paper airplane play, in my experience, consists generally of accuracy and duration challenges—carefully landing where intended from as far away as possible. A fun iterative process of build, fly, redesign, build, fly, and try again.

43 | Traditional Paper Dart

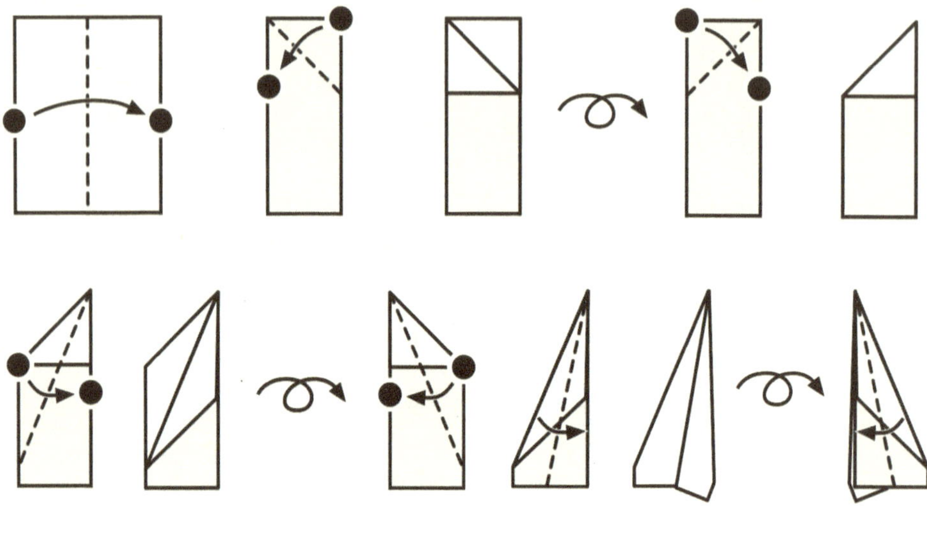

THE PAPER DART.

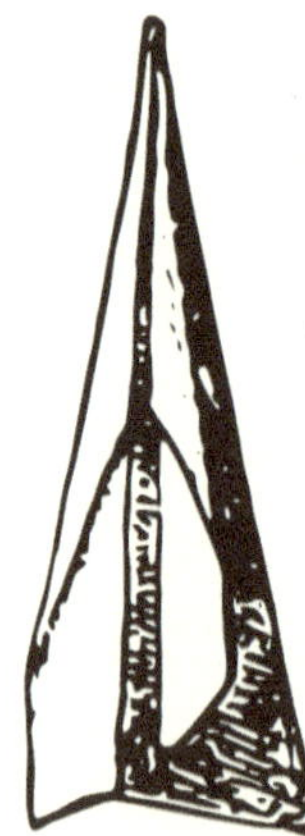

To form this dart you must take an oblong piece of paper, and fold it down the middle lengthwise; then double each of the lower corners up to the middle crease, and fold the doubled paper over to the same mark; you must now turn each folded side outwards, and your dart will resemble the annexed figure. The paper dart when thrown from the hand rarely hits the object aimed at, as it generally makes a graceful curve in passing through the air. Boys sometimes amuse themselves by fighting sham battles with these harmless weapons.

1859.

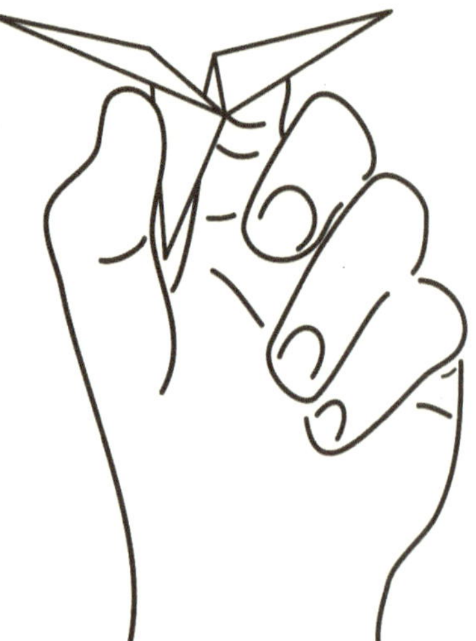

A traditional design, this is the paper airplane my grandmother taught me, my introduction to paper folding.

The first known illustration and description of how to make this appears to be in the book "Games and Sports for Young Boys," published 1859 in London by Routledge, Warne, and Routledge.

This basic design was understood by readers to be a projectile—a dart—thrown at targets. It was some time before this dart became a paper airplane.

Sir George Cayley (1773-1857) described the fundamentals of modern aircraft design in 1799. The first powered manned flight by the Wright brothers took place in 1903.

"The whole problem is confined within these limits, viz. to make a surface support a given weight by the application of power to the resistance of air."
Sir George Cayley, "On Aerial Navigation," Nicholson's Journal of Natural Philosophy, Chemistry and the Arts 25 (1809).

41 | Paper Airplane from Square

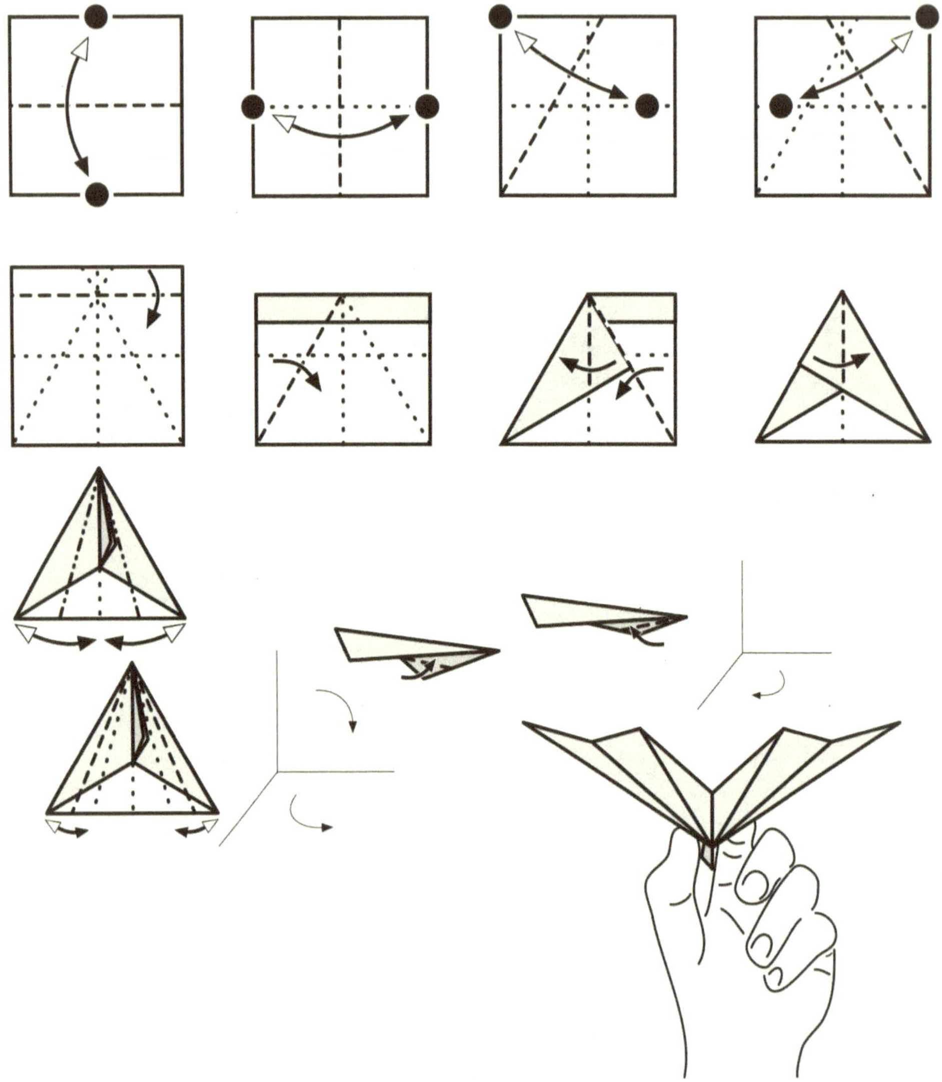

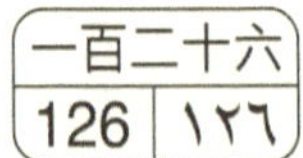

Simple folds provide an elegant glider with a weighted nose locked in place by a folded ventral, downward or belly, fin.

One corner is folded down, then the other, and an equilateral triangle appears. These two creases intersect just below the top edge of the paper. This defines the crease parallel to the top edge. Next, the top corners are folded back down on the existing creases.

The overlapping corners are then folded back out, with these valley creases made along the central top to bottom crease. These corners should now stand up, perpendicular to the plane of the main triangle. This will become the ventral fin.

From figure nine, the side edges are folded in to meet the center line. These mountain folds are then unfolded. The side edges are now folded in to those creases and these valley folds are unfolded.

The form is now rotated as shown and two intersecting valley folds are made in the ventral fin.

15 | Paper Airplane, Long Dart, from Rectangle

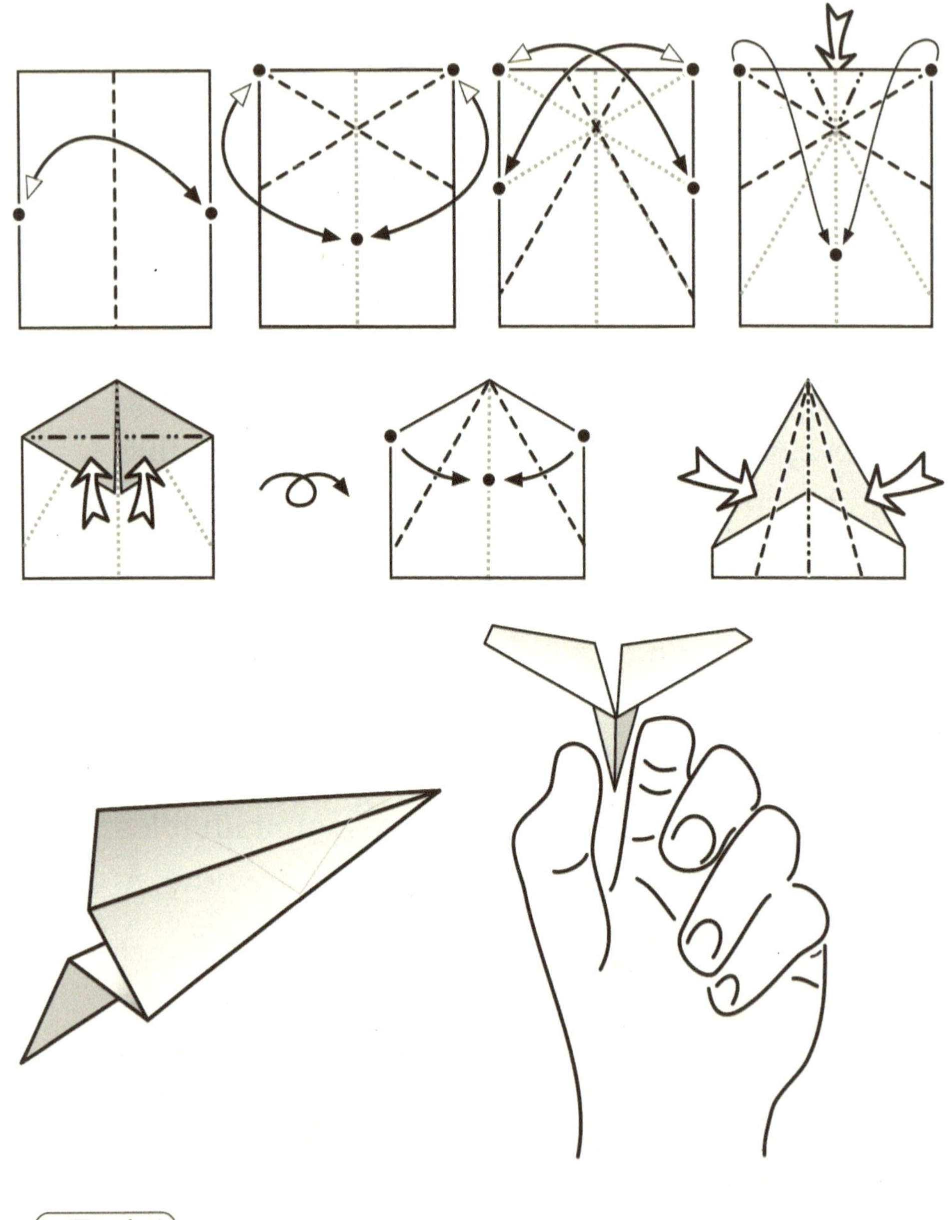

Here is presented another triangle based glider, in this instance starting from a rectangle.

In the first figure the paper is folded in half and unfolded. Next the top corners are each folded down, and then unfolded, such that the corner meets the middle crease and the crease formed originates at the other corner. It's like starting to fold a triangle from the rectangle. These creases then define the points where the corners next fold to meet, and are unfolded.

In the fourth figure a section of two creases is refolded as mountain folds, and a section of two other creases are folded as valley folds. These are all folded simultaneously, pushing the middle of top edge down as the top corners come down and fold over. The fifth figure shows these corners tucked down and back under.

Flipping the entire form over, the sides are folded in to the center finalizing the shape of the plane. The wings are defined as they are pushed in toward the center.

14 | Paper Airplane, Symmetrical from Rectangle

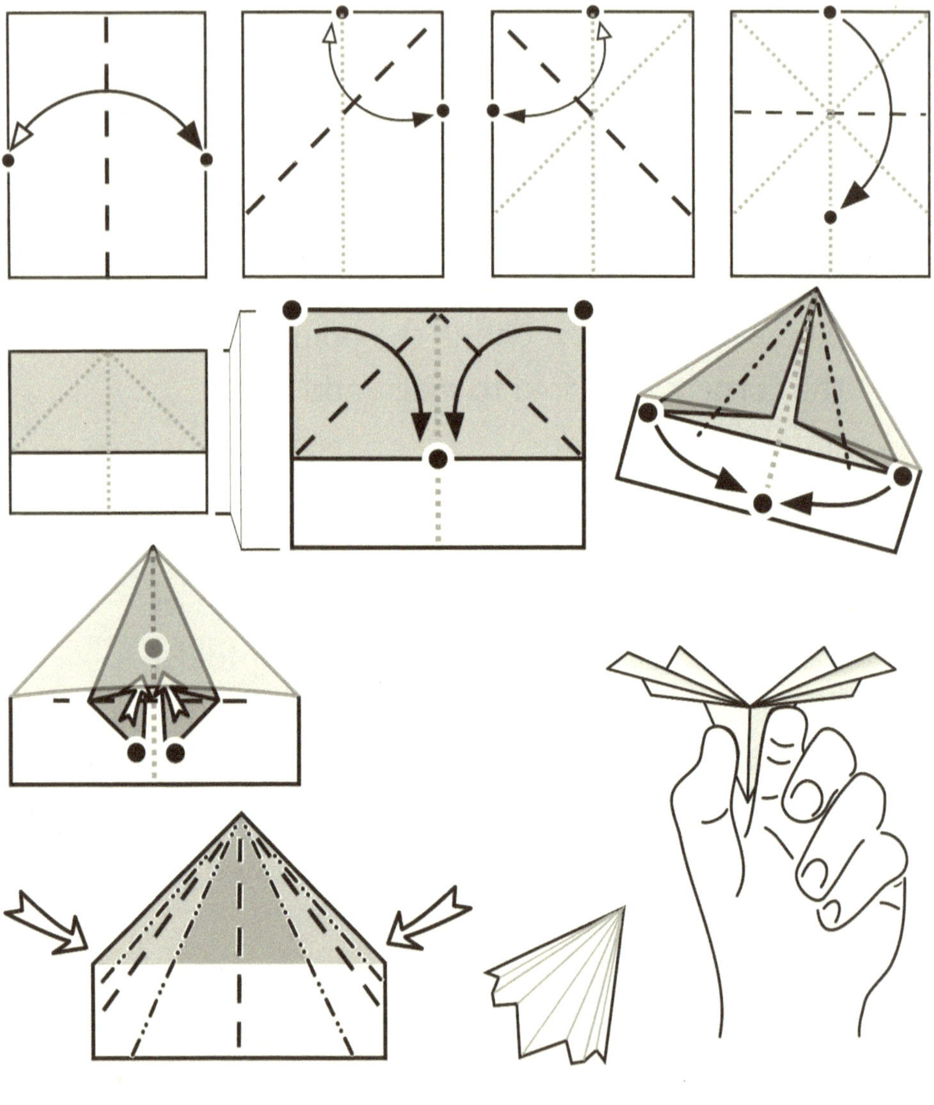

Presented here is a symmetrical triangular airplane. Front heavy, this design flies fast and straight.

With the folds locked into place in the next to last step, the design is stable without the need for any fasteners.

This is a recent design based on my very first original design, which is presented next in this collection.

Folding begins with a central fold followed by the top two corners folded down, then unfolded. At their intersection, the top is folded down, then the top corners are folded down.

In figure seven the corners inside are folded under in a twisting motion.

Figure eight shows how the extending corners are folded up and back into the pocket, locking the design in place.

The wings are then folded up and down, each fold being halfway between the previous creases.

13 | Paper Airplane from Rectangle

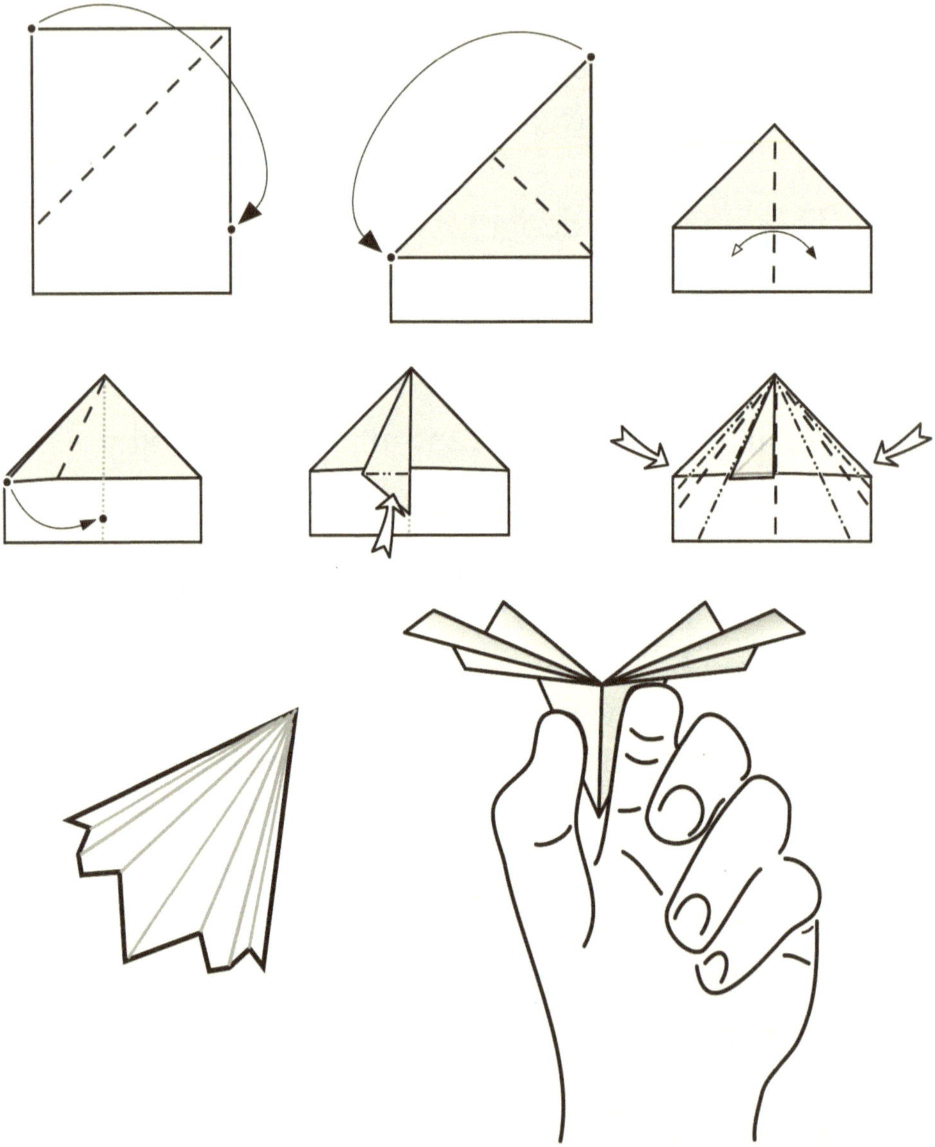

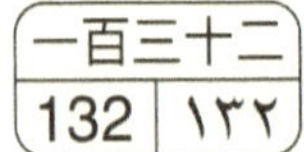

Published:
Pacific Coast OrigamiUSA
Conference 2023
Page 11

Sitting at the dining room table with my grandmother, in our origami hangar working on the next paper airplane, we would always have staples in the Swingline Tot 50 and there was always a roll of 3M Scotch Magic Tape. When I was home or at school, I did not have this reliable resource. This was at least in part my motivation, to design a paper airplane that requires no fasteners or tape, and can be folded using standard letter size or A4 copy paper, or any paper with roughly 4:3 proportions.

In 2009, I published my first book, Fluffy the Vulture (ISBN 9780615266879). This plane mimics the flying of Fluffy the Vulture, whose wings also form a "V" shape.
"let the wings be inclined to each other, so as to form an angle... secures the stability"
Sir George Cayley, "On Aerial Navigation," Nicholson's Journal of Natural Philosophy, Chemistry and the Arts 24 (1809).

Also by the author...

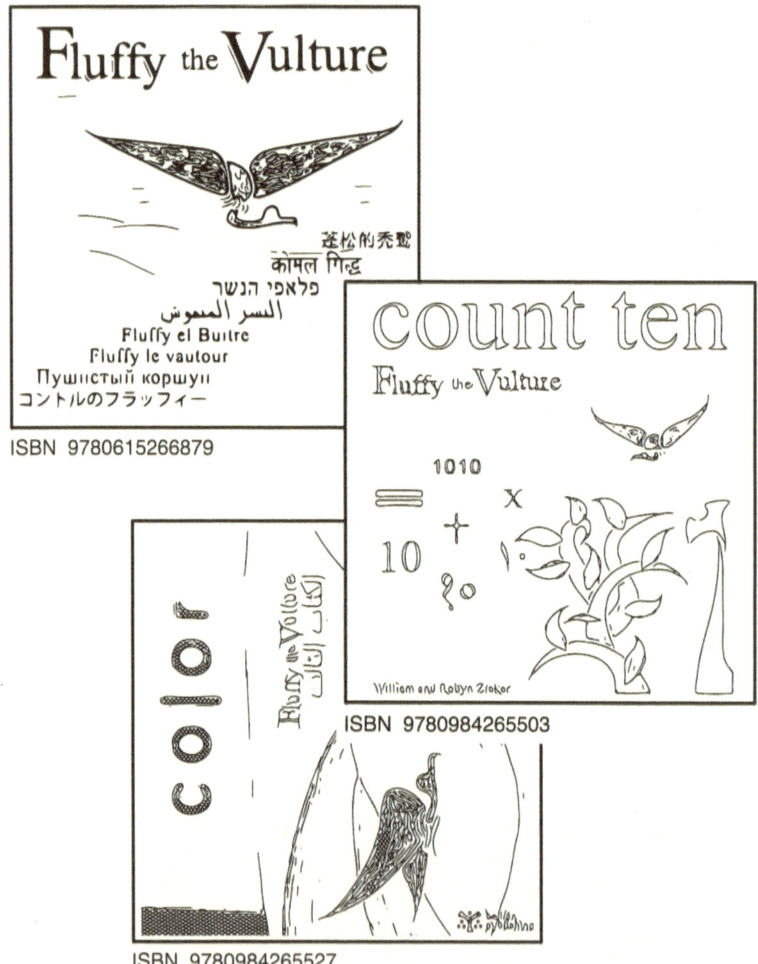

ISBN 9780615266879

ISBN 9780984265503

ISBN 9780984265527

Appropriate Technology Malaria Vector Control

"Approximately 95% of the ⟦estimated 597,000⟧ deaths ⟦from malaria worldwide in 2023⟧ occurred in the WHO African Region, where many at risk still lack access to the services they need to prevent, detect and treat the disease." United Nations, World Health Organization, World malaria report 2024

"⟦Appropriate technology is⟧ small scale, energy efficient, environmentally sound, labor intensive, and controlled by the local community ⟦and⟧ must be simple enough to be maintained by the people using it." Field Guide to Appropriate Technology, Academic Press, 2003

Sweat related volatile organic compounds (VOCs) attract mosquitoes that transmit disease. Made with only starch and water and working through cohesion, novel starch gel dramatically reduces interaction of the skin microbiome and apocrine sweat. VOC production is reduced, potentially hiding one from mosquitoes. Made locally using available materials.

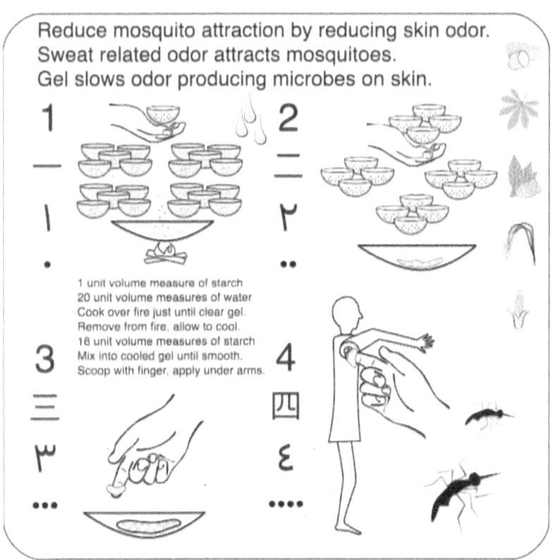

Music.

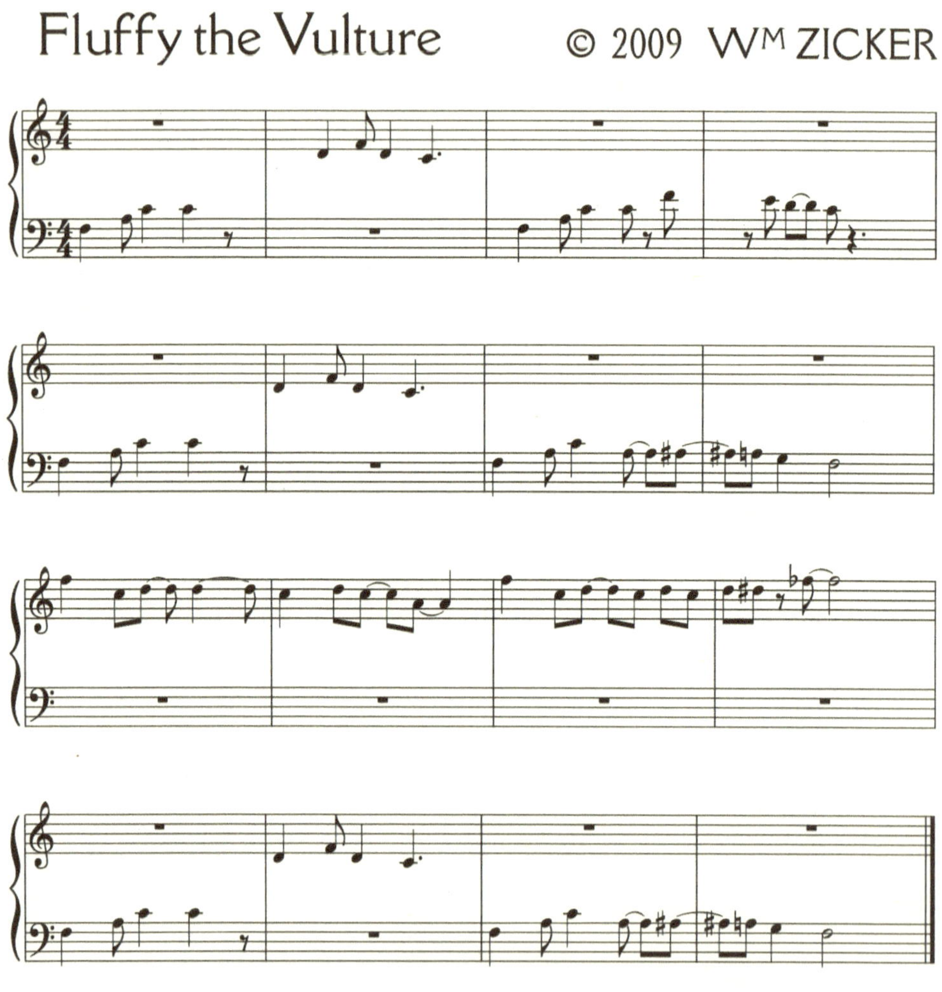

O! Alphabet

© W[M] ZICKER

Oh... P Q R S T U V W X Y Z

A B C D E F G H I J KLM N!

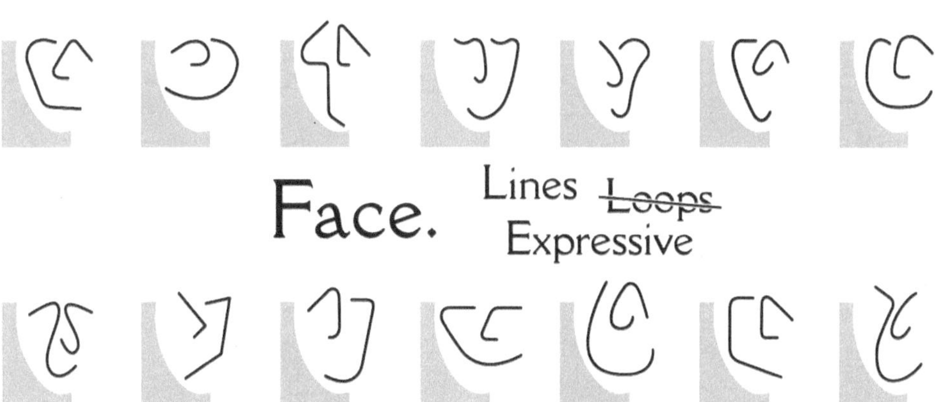

Hands

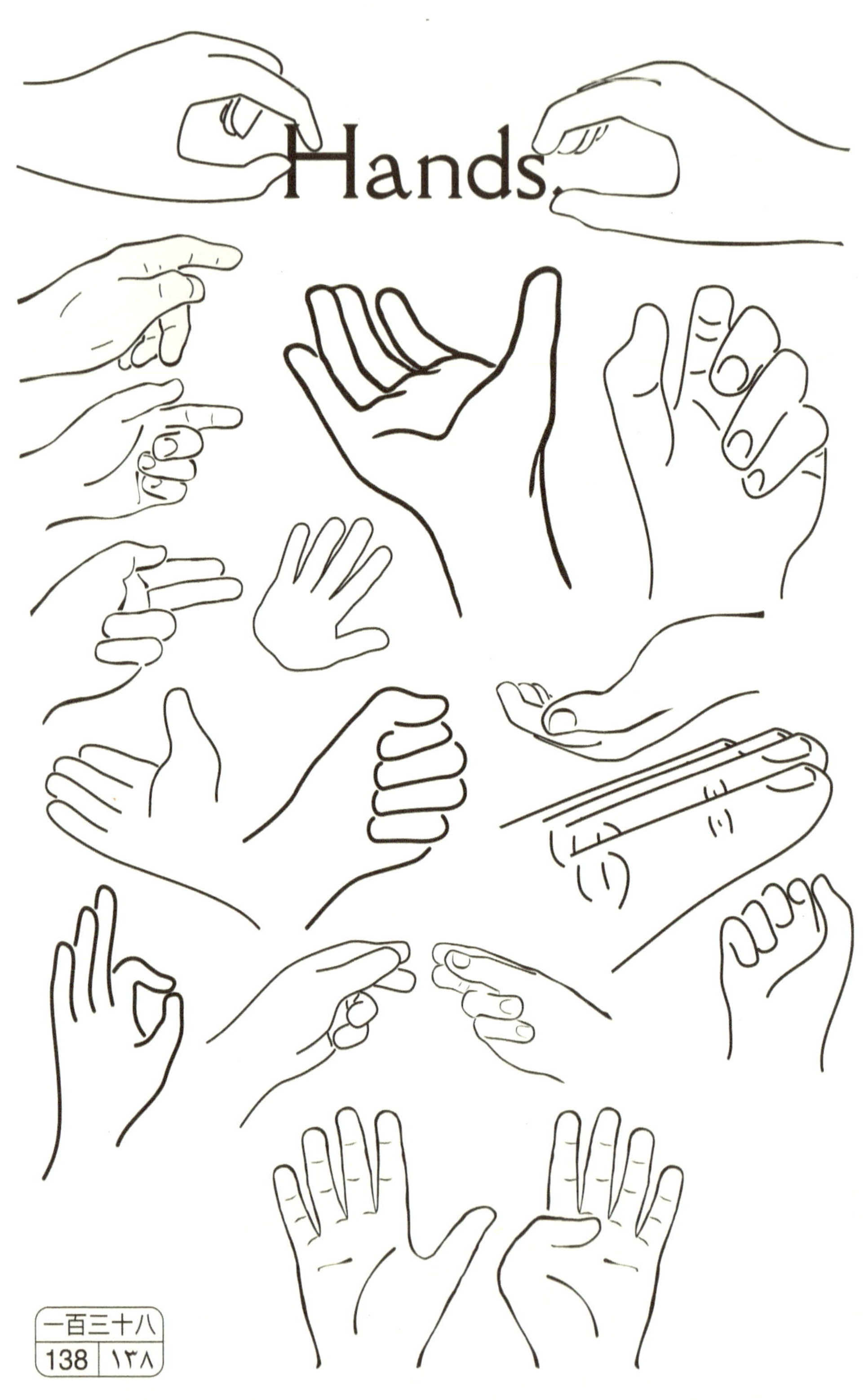

what do you call
a deer that
eats spiders?

a web browser

www.ingramcontent.com/pod-product-compliance
Lightning Source LLC
LaVergne TN
LVHW051006080826
845145LV00009B/2478

* 9 7 8 0 9 8 4 2 6 5 5 3 4 *